# the rewilding year

# Contents

| | |
|---|---:|
| Introduction | 1 |
| Who this book is for and how to use it. | 5 |
| What is "Rewilding" anyway? | 8 |
| Moon-manifesting | 11 |
| Women wild (poem) | 23 |
| Sound Healing | 24 |
| A whisper wild (poem) | 33 |
| Earthing | 34 |
| Small nature (poem) | 41 |
| Speaking with nature | 42 |
| The wild woman archetype (essay) | 56 |
| Wild swimming | 59 |
| The path (poem) | 68 |
| Crafting remedies | 69 |
| Unplugging from social media: a wild return to presence (essay) | 84 |
| Nature journaling | 87 |
| All The Beauty That I See (poem) | 94 |
| Healing the land | 95 |
| How to heal the sister wound (essay) | 102 |
| Rewilding the body | 106 |
| Granddaughters of witches (poem) | 114 |
| Studying the sky | 115 |
| Lost and found (poem) | 121 |
| Wintering | 122 |
| Pitter-patter (poem) | 130 |
| Solo-adventuring | 131 |
| Leaving it all behind (poem) | 136 |
| Letting o: How My Own Rewilding Year Came to an Unexpected Close | 137 |
| Author's note | 139 |
| Sources & inspiration | 140 |

*I would like to acknowledge the Wadandi People of Western Australia, the traditional custodians past and present of the land from where I write my stories.*

# Introduction

Let me start by saying that you do not need this book. Everything you need to rewild your life is available to you right here and now, for free. You don't need any tools; you don't need my words to guide you. All you have to do to rewild your life is go outside and listen.

Listen until the noise inside you settles. Let the rustle of leaves remind you how to breathe, and the movement of clouds show you that nothing stays still for long. Let the soil stain your hands and the wind rearrange your thoughts. Rewilding begins the moment you remember that you belong to the world, not apart from it. It asks for attention, not effort, presence, not mastery. When you start to listen in this way, you realise that nature has been speaking all along, waiting for you to answer.

Having said all that, why does this book exist, then? Simply put: Because I have thoroughly enjoyed making it. This book is a labour of love that I indulged in on weekends and late nights, or when I needed a break from my regular writing work. And while I mean it when I say, you do not need this book, that's not to say I don't believe it provides value.

The value of this book lies in its practicality for the modern woman who is often stretched thin by the demands of work, family, and the endless lists of "shoulds." Many women feel the pull to reconnect with something deeper, yet don't know where to begin, and that's usually how people find me online, searching for information on the "How." In 2024, I decided to make a personal rewilding experiment. It began with a hunch. A small spark of an idea that found me on a walk one afternoon. At first, it seemed nothing more than a passing thought, but it grew. It grew into a plan for an entire year of my life. To hold myself accountable, I recorded a podcast project I called **My Rewilding Year** – twelve magical months of learning how to reconnect with nature, step by step, in the midst of ordinary life. **What has always drawn me is the idea of wildness itself – not just as a landscape, but as a way of being.**

I have long been fascinated by what happens when we step outside of the boundaries of the lives we've constructed and let the rawness of the natural world touch us. Wildness offers a mirror that shows me who I am beneath the layers of expectation and performance. Even before I had words for it, I felt a magnetic pull toward places where the edges are rough, where the rules are different, where life is stripped back to its essentials. My rewilding year, then, wasn't my first encounter with wildness: When I was twenty-seven, I packed up my life in Germany, where I had worked as a Berlin-based tv-producer throughout my twenties, and journeyed to South Africa to train as a safari- and trails guide. I spent a year walking (often barefoot) in the African bush, sleeping in tents, and learning how to approach elephants, lions, and buffalo on foot.

That year cracked me open. It taught me what it feels like to be absorbed into wildness completely, to belong to the earth in a way I had never known before. But that wasn't the beginning, either. The longing that carried me there had been growing. For years, I travelled whenever I had been able to save up some money, spent a year in Australia on a work and travel visa, and discovered how much I loved writing. But through it all, one longing grew louder than everything else: I wanted to be outside. **I wanted to feel the ground under my feet.** I wanted to use my hands, to learn how to make a fire from scratch, to live close to earth. That longing is what finally brought me to the South African bush.

And yet, as wild and extraordinary as the safari guide training was, it was also, in a way, easy. A quick fix. An *outer* change. Because when you place yourself in the middle of wildness, wildness *will* claim you. The harder part, I would soon discover, is carrying it back home. The harder part is keeping the thread alive in ordinary life – at a desk, in four walls, paying bills, doing the everyday.

That is where this book begins.

Because what I have come to understand is this: **Wild is a way of being.** For me, it has two strands. One is the rewilding of the self, the inner journey of loosening the story of separation we've been told, of choosing to go outside, to reconnect, to remember that we are part of a whole. The other is the rewilding of the land itself: acknowledging what has been broken and daring to repair it. Together they form the work of rewilding the soul.

When I left the African continent at the start of the pandemic, I lost my "easy access" to wildness. Without the elephants, I had to relearn how to find it here, in my new home in Australia, where I moved to be with my husband in 2020. That's when I realised you cannot just change your surroundings and expect to be transformed. You have to do the inner work. You cannot just walk into a library and expect to know the books. You have to sit down and read them, too. And so, I began again. I wrote down practices, small, simple, wild things I wanted to weave into my days for one entire year, one practice for each month. Things that might draw me closer to the moon, to water, to silence, to earth. That list became the seed of this book.

At first, I thought it was just for me, a journal to keep me accountable. But then the idea began to take shape. **What if there was a guide, a companion, a workbook for a rewilding year?** What if it could offer rhythm and prompts, not to prescribe but to invite? What if it could be co-written by each reader, scribbled in, pressed with flowers, made wholly their own? That is what you are holding now.

Your rewilding year will not look like mine. And it shouldn't. You may take more than twelve months. You may skip challenges, reorder them, or create your own. That is exactly how it should be. The true work of rewilding is to trust your own knowing.

So, let this book be more than paper and ink. Let it be a confidant, a companion, a place you can return to, again and again. And while you do this work, know that you are not alone in your longing. Many of us feel it. Many of us *are* remembering. And together, we are reclaiming what has been lost.

Personally, I think every woman should go on a Rewilding Year once in her lifetime. Answer the call. Howl with the wolves. Embark on that pilgrimage to who she truly is deep down. If this book hopes to do anything at all, it would be to encourage more of us to actually go out and do it.

Think of this as a wild gap year for the soul. You don't need to quit your job or move to the wilderness to begin. You can start right here, right now.

**The wilderness is waiting.**

# Who this book is for and how to use it.

This book is for women who feel the quiet tug of something ancient stirring inside them. Women who stand under the moon and feel, deep in their bones, that they were once meant to live in rhythm with their cycles. Women who long for a way of being that is slower, softer, and ultimately: *wilder*.

It is for the ones who sense that something has been lost. That our modern lives, so full of schedules and screens, have buried a deeper knowing: The wisdom of listening to the land. The wisdom of gathering in circles. The wisdom of herbs, of water, of wild things. Forgotten ways that our grandmothers' grandmothers once held close.

You may not have words for this longing, only the ache of knowing there must be more than rushing, producing, and striving. You may feel guilty for wanting more, when your life already looks "full enough." Yet the call persists. It comes in dreams, in moments of stillness, in the way your body relaxes when your feet touch the earth.

If you are here, you have already heard it. That whisper, that calling back. This book is your companion as you remember who you were always meant to be.

## How to use this book:

All twelve practices are introduced now so that you can prepare in advance. Some will be simple to begin straight away. Others may take time… gathering herbs, finding a local teacher, planning a retreat, or even taking time away from work for the final practice, the Solo Adventure.

The monthly practices are arranged in an order that balances outward, active experiences with inward, contemplative ones. Some challenges build gently on one another. For instance, "Sound Healing" creates a foundation for "Speaking with Nature". Earthing is best in warmer months, "Wintering" belongs… well, in winter. And "Skygazing" works well in a season of clearer skies. "Wild Swimming" can be done any time of year, though your body may have very different experiences in icy water versus summer waves.

Woven between the monthly practices, you'll find essays about ideas and topics I contemplated, as well as poems I wrote during my own rewilding year. The latter have never been shared with anyone, and I don't know, but there's something about poetry that feels extra-raw to me, vulnerable to the core. I really hope you'll like them…

## The twelve practices (in my suggested order):

- Moon-manifesting
- Earthing
- Sound healing
- Speaking with nature
- Wild swimming
- Crafting remedies
- Keeping a nature journal
- Healing the land
- Rewilding the body
- Sky-gazing
- Wintering
- Solo-adventuring

Each chapter introduces a practice to engage with during that particular month, offers stories from my own journey, and then invites you to step into it in your own way, providing practical tools, guidance and further reading. Once you have completed a month, you might like to colour the mandala behind each title, to keep track of your progress. You are encouraged to scribble notes in the margins, press flowers, paste feathers, and make this book fully your own.

And that is perhaps the most important thing to know: this book, this journey, is **not about learning something new. Rather, it's trying to help you remember something old.** Remember that women once lived with the rhythms of the earth, the phases of the moon, the wisdom of plants and the seasons. Remember that we once knew how to listen, how to trust our intuition, how to *belong*. You see, or maybe you even feel that distinction? This stuff is not knowledge to be studied. It is wisdom to be reawakened.

So, let this book be a companion on your journey of remembering. One year of wonder, stillness, and rediscovery. One year of stepping back into who you already are, and who women have always been… starts *now*.

# What is "Rewilding" anyway?

The word Rewilding first belonged to conservationists. It described the daring idea of giving land back to itself. In Yellowstone National Park, it meant bringing wolves home after seventy years of absence. People feared what might happen; yet when the wolves returned, the entire landscape shifted. Deer moved differently, plants regenerated, birds nested in new growth. All because one keystone animal was allowed to come back. Stories like these sparked a movement. Forests began to be restored. Wetlands refilled. Species returned to places that had been silent for decades. Scientists saw the wisdom in letting nature lead again.

But the word didn't stay in the realm of science; it slipped out into the wider world. It began to appear in books, in circles of women, in conversations held over tea. Because on some level, many of us already knew this isn't only meant for wolves and forests. It's for us, too. **We have been tamed, managed, and trimmed just as landscapes have.** We've been pushed into neat rows, told to work to the clock, to ignore the moon and the seasons of our own bodies. And just like the Earth, something in us longs to return. So, when I speak of rewilding, I speak of two faces. The rewilding of the land. And the rewilding of the soul.

## Rewilding the land

To rewild land is to trust that life remembers itself. It doesn't always take a grand project. It can begin in the smallest of ways: Let a corner of your garden grow into a tangle of grasses and flowers, and you'll soon find bees and butterflies making it their home. Plant native herbs or wildflowers in a pot on a balcony, and suddenly you are feeding entire lineages of pollinators. Leave a bowl of water outside, and the birds may find it by dawn.

These are acts of welcome, of returning space. And from there, the ripples widen: volunteering with local rewilding groups, planting trees, signing petitions for wilder policies, choosing companies that protect instead of extract. Each of these choices is like dropping a seed. Some sprout right before your eyes, others take longer, but all matter. **When we step back, the Earth steps forward.** And when she does, she astonishes us with how quickly she can heal.

*"It's no accident that this systematic suppression of the feminine has been accompanied down the centuries not only by the devaluation of all that is wild and instinctual in our own natures, but by the purposeful destruction of natural ecosystems. We long ago turned our backs on the planet which gives us life."*

Sharon Blackie, "If Women Rose Rooted"

## Rewilding the soul

But the wild does not live only outside. It is inside us, too. For centuries, women especially have been told to silence the instinctual. To be polite, to be neat, to put away their wild laugh or their sharp intuition. We've been told to make ourselves smaller, smoother, easier. And yet, something deep in our bones still remembers another way of being. Rewilding the soul is listening to that memory. It might look like walking alone in the woods until your body relaxes into its own rhythm. Or writing in a journal as though you are speaking to the Earth herself and hearing her answer back.

It might be dancing barefoot in your kitchen or lying on the grass at night until you can pick out the rhythm of the crickets. Sometimes it comes through knowledge, learning the names of the trees you walk past, or the herbs that grow at your feet. Other times it comes through *unknowing*, through silence, prayer, or surrender. It comes through tending the body like the wild creature it is: stretching, lifting, eating in ways that give you strength. There is no one way. But there *is* one truth: the wild in you is not gone. It waits patiently for you to remember.

## The two faces together

The land heals as we heal. And we heal as the land heals. These two faces of rewilding are inseparable. If we pour our energy only into ecological work but never tend to our own inner exhaustion, we will keep repeating the same patterns of domination. If we tend only to ourselves and ignore the burning forests, the rivers choked with plastic, our healing remains cut off from the whole. Together, though, something shifts. Plant a seed, and you feel your own heart steady. Walk barefoot on the earth, and you sense how urgently she longs to be free again. Each gesture in one direction nourishes the other. Rewilding, then, is not a trend or a hobby. It is a remembering of how to live in relationship, how to listen again, how to trust. **It is both outer work and inner work, both soil and soul.** Most of all, it is *ongoing*. It cannot be ticked off a list. It must be lived, day by day, season by season.

## An invitation

Rewilding is bigger than a project, smaller than a lifetime, and exactly the size of this moment. It can begin right where you are: with a plant on your windowsill, with a single deep breath outside, with a decision to spend more time listening than striving. As you move through this book, you'll be invited to touch both faces of rewilding. Some practices will draw you outwards, into rivers, into community, into the sky. Others will draw you inwards, into journaling, stillness, or rest. Each one is a thread, and together they form the weaving of a wilder life.

**The Earth remembers. And so do you.**

## Manifesting with the moon phases

Welcome to your very first practice of the year. Each month, we will explore one ritual, one rhythm, one way of returning to the wildness that is already within you. And we begin with one of the oldest, simplest, and most universal companions humans have ever known: the moon.

Now, I know the word "manifesting" has gotten a bit of a bad reputation in recent years. To some, it sounds like magical thinking, wishful daydreaming, or a social media trend. But I'd like to invite you to reconsider. At its heart, manifesting simply means living with intention, choosing consciously what you want to invite into your life, and then aligning your actions with that vision. That's it. And when we place this practice within the cycle of the moon, it becomes less about chasing dreams and more about reconnecting with a rhythm as old as the earth itself.

If the word manifesting makes you cringe, that's worth paying attention to. I've learned that when a word or idea triggers me, there is usually something underneath it that wants to be explored. Why does it make us uncomfortable to name what we want? Why does it feel awkward to say our hopes out loud? Often, it's because we've been taught to downplay our desires, or to believe they are frivolous. But when we begin to honour them, when we say them clearly, and then take aligned action, something is allowed to shift: We stop drifting, and we begin to live deliberately. That is what manifesting with the moon is really about.

Now, why the moon? Because the moon offers us a natural calendar, a visible cycle of waxing and waning that mirrors the human, and especially the female, experience. Just as the moon grows, shines, and retreats, so too do we expand, create, reflect, and let go. Aligning our actions with the moon is noticing and participating in this cycle of becoming. It keeps us accountable, steady, and connected, to our goals, and to the living world around us. Think of the moon as your guide. Each one of its phases offers a cue: when to plant seeds of intention, when to take action, when to celebrate your progress, and when to release what no longer serves you. By learning to tune into these phases, you begin to live not by the clock or the calendar anymore, but also by the rhythms of the earth and sky. This practice is as practical as it is mystical. It will keep you on track, yes. But more than that, it will remind you that you are part of a much larger cycle of growth and renewal. So, let's begin where the moon always begins: the New Moon.

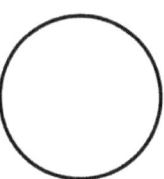

**New Moon: Planting seeds**

Every cycle begins in darkness. The sky looks empty, the moon invisible, and yet beneath that black canvas something is already stirring. This is the paradox of the New Moon: it is both nothing and everything at once. A blank page. A quiet soil. A threshold.

For thousands of years, people have looked to this moment to begin anew. Farmers sowed seeds when the nights were darkest. Poets and mystics wrote of death and rebirth. And today, in our lives filled with notifications and deadlines, the New Moon still offers us that same invitation: to pause, to listen, to plant our own intentions. The New Moon asks you to stop doing, take a beat, and start tuning in. It is the perfect reminder that growth always begins unseen. Just as roots stretch quietly under the earth before a sprout ever emerges, your dreams begin in silence, long before they take shape in the outer world. This phase teaches us patience, trust, and the courage to begin again, no matter how many times we've "failed" before. Living by the New Moon also helps break the illusion that time is linear. It reminds us that life is cyclical, that we always have another chance to reset. If last month didn't unfold the way you hoped, here is your fresh start.

## A new moon ritual

I firmly believe that rituals don't need to be complicated. What matters most is your presence. Here's one way you might step into the energy of the New Moon:

- Prepare your space. Dim the lights, light a candle, spread a blanket on the floor. Create a nook that feels safe, intentional, free from interruption.

- Get quiet. Take a few minutes to breathe deeply or meditate. Imagine the busy energy of the day draining out of you, leaving you clear and receptive.

- Journal your intentions. Ask yourself:
    - What do I want to invite into my life this month?
    - What do I need to release to make space for it?
    - If nothing stood in my way, what would I choose?

- - Write your answers as affirmations beginning with "I am…" (I am grounded. I am creative. I am ready for love.).
- Speak them aloud. This is the part that feels strange at first, but it changes everything. By giving your words sound, you make them real.

Once you've set your intentions, keep them close. Write them on a piece of paper you tuck under your pillow or place them on your nightstand or desk. Look at them throughout the month, but don't become attached. These are your seeds. You don't need to force them to grow; you only need to tend them. And when the moon begins to wax, your role will shift from dreaming to doing. But for now, in the darkness of the New Moon, your task is simple: be still, be clear, and dare to name what you truly want.

**Waxing crescent & first quarter moon: taking first steps**

If the New Moon is the seed planted in the dark soil, the Waxing Crescent is the very first sprout breaking through. Something fragile yet determined is reaching for light. This is the phase of beginnings-in-motion, of carrying your intention out of your journal and into the world. After the stillness of the New Moon, the waxing crescent and first quarter moons stir us back into action. Energy begins to build. You may notice you feel more motivated, more curious, or more willing to try something new. This is the time to honour your intentions by moving toward them, even if it's just a small step. It is easy to get stuck in dreaming, to wait for the "perfect" moment to begin. But this moon reminds us: the perfect moment is now. The crescent moon does not hesitate to grow, it simply begins, little by little, night after night. Your task is the same. Think of this as the phase of courage. Just as the young sprout risks breaking through the soil, you too must risk beginning. It is not about perfection. It is about momentum.

## A waxing crescent ritual

You don't need hours of ceremony here because this is a working moon, a *doing* moon. Here's a simple practice to align yourself with its energy:

- Return to your intentions. Look back at what you wrote during the New Moon. Which one speaks loudest right now? Which one feels most ready for action?

- Choose a first step. Keep it small. If your intention was "I am creative", your first step might be buying paints or opening a fresh notebook. If your intention was "I am fit and healthy", it might mean lacing up your shoes for a short walk.

- Act. Do the thing. Don't overthink it. Don't wait for the mood to strike. Begin now, however imperfectly. And don't stop there: This is the time for new routines, for consistency, for repetition. It's not easy, but it's worth it.

## The first quarter moon: meeting resistance? – You bet.

Roughly a week after the New Moon, the First Quarter arrives: a half moon in the sky. Half illuminated, half shadowed, it symbolises tension. This is the moment in the cycle when obstacles often appear. Suddenly, your new intention may feel harder to pursue. Doubt creeps in. Life throws you curveballs. Don't be discouraged. **This resistance is part of the rhythm.** Just as a young plant pushes against stones in the soil, your intention will meet its first challenges. The First Quarter teaches persistence. It asks: How much do you want this? What will you do when it gets difficult? During this phase, keep showing up. Take small, consistent steps, and celebrate each one. When resistance appears, see it not as failure but as initiation. Every new path asks us to prove our commitment. For me, a useful mantra for this phase is:

**Follow the journey. Trust the process.**

# Waxing gibbous moon: momentum builds

If the New Moon is a seed and the Waxing Crescent is the fragile sprout, the Waxing Gibbous is when the plant takes shape, stretching tall, gathering strength, and preparing to flower. This is a phase of growth that feels both exhilarating and demanding. Energy is high, opportunities present themselves, and progress becomes visible.

The Waxing Gibbous arrives just before the Full Moon, and it carries that same bright, pulsing energy... but it is still just that: *waxing*, building. This is not completion, but acceleration. If you tune in attentively, you may feel a rush of ideas, invitations, or synchronicities. Things begin to click into place. If you've been consistent with your actions since the New Moon, this is often the time you see some first results.

But with growth also comes pressure. The Waxing Gibbous can also feel overwhelming, as if there's suddenly too much happening at once. You might feel stretched thin, juggling too many projects, or buzzing with nervous excitement. This is natural. Think of it as a reminder that energy is moving, and you are in the thick of creation.

## Navigating the energy

At this point in the moon's cycle, you are asked to do two things at once:

- Keep building. Stay committed to your intentions and actions.

- Refine. Notice what's working and what's not and make adjustments before the Full Moon arrives.

The Waxing Gibbous is like a dress rehearsal before opening night. It's the chance to polish, fine-tune, and prepare yourself to step into fullness.

## A waxing gibbous ritual

This is a phase of alignment, of ensuring your actions match your intentions. Here's a practice you can try:

- Review your progress. Sit down with your New Moon intentions and your journal. Ask: What has moved forward since then? Where am I already seeing growth?

- Identify obstacles. Where am I meeting resistance? What feels heavy or draining? Write these down without judgment.

- Refine your focus. Cross out what no longer feels alive. Circle the goals or intentions that still spark energy. Add any new insights that have emerged in the past weeks.

- Take aligned action. Choose one concrete step that supports your strongest intention right now. Do it today, while the energy is high.

This is a phase of optimism, momentum, but also of accountability. It rewards persistence, but it also teaches discernment. Not everything you set in motion at the New Moon will be worth carrying forward. The Waxing Gibbous reminds you that it's okay – even wise – to refine your course. Celebrate the wins, however small. Notice how far you've come since the darkness of the New Moon. And remember you are preparing to meet the Full Moon, the culmination, the harvest, the brightest moment of the cycle.

A mantra for this phase:

**I trust the process of growth. I adjust with grace.**

# Full moon: illumination & release

The Full Moon is the crown of the lunar cycle. After weeks of building, stretching, and striving, the moon has reached her brightest moment, glowing in full splendour. Nothing is hidden now; every curve illuminated, every shadow banished. And we, too, are invited into this clarity.

The Full Moon is both a celebration and a reckoning. On the one hand, it is a time of joy, a chance to acknowledge what has blossomed since the New Moon, to honour the progress you've made, and to marvel at the ways life has unfolded. On the other hand, its brightness makes visible the things that are not working. Patterns that hold you back. Habits that no longer serve. Fears and blockages that lurk in the corners of your mind.

This duality is what makes the Full Moon so potent: it gives us both light and shadow. It offers us the chance to say yes to what we wish to keep, and no to what we are ready to release.

## The energy of the full moon

Many people notice their bodies and emotions respond strongly during the Full Moon. Sleep may be restless, thoughts may whirl, creativity may surge. You might feel overstimulated, buzzing with ideas, or unusually sensitive. This is not in your head. Countless cultures across the world have observed how Full Moons stir the tides, the animals, and the human spirit.

Instead of resisting this intensity, you can choose to work with it. Think of it as fuel: wild, bright, and overflowing. Your task is to direct it with intention.

## A full moon ritual

Here's one way to harness the fullness:

- Find your centre. Sit somewhere quiet. If possible, go outside and let the moonlight touch your skin. If clouds hide it, a photograph of the moon will do; intention matters more than setting. Take a few slow, cleansing breaths.

- Reflect. Open your journal and write freely. Pour out your thoughts, your emotions, your ideas. Don't censor yourself. This is a time for overflow.

- Celebrate. Look back at your New Moon intentions. What has taken root? What small or large victories have unfolded? Write them down. Honour yourself for showing up.

- Release. On a separate piece of paper, write down what feels heavy, blocked, or no longer aligned. When finished, destroy the paper: burn it in a fire-safe vessel, tear it into tiny pieces, or let it flow away in water. The symbolic act matters: you are declaring your readiness to let go.

- Offer gratitude. Speak or write what you are thankful for, not only the things you've received, but also the lessons, the challenges, and the clarity.

The Full Moon reminds us that we do not grow in a straight line. We grow in cycles of expansion and contraction, of fullness and release. Each month, the Full Moon gives us the gift of closure: a chance to reset before beginning again. A mantra for this phase:

**I celebrate my growth. I release what no longer serves me.**

The moon will soon begin to wane, and your energy will turn inward again. For now, stay with this fullness. Stand under the sky, breathe deeply, and remember that like the moon, you are capable of shining fully, even after darkness.

I want to be clear here, though: I don't do this every month. Life is busy, and sometimes the days blur past without a single ritual. What I've learned, though, is that even one month of living with the moon can change how you see it forever. Once you've followed a cycle from seed to fullness, you start to notice the sky differently. You look up and know where you are in the rhythm. That awareness doesn't disappear, and that's the whole idea behind The Rewilding Year. We're not striving for perfection here: we're trying to create a new awareness, a new way of being.

You don't need candles and ceremonies each time. You don't need to dance naked and wolf-howl under *every* full moon… although, if you feel called to, I am all for that. What matters is knowing the moon is there. That you can turn to it when things feel uncertain, when you long for clarity, or when you need a reminder that cycles of growth and release are natural.

I find that, in general, just knowing how to ask for things is so important, and the more I venture down this wild path, the more I trust to ask not just the people in my life for help or advice, but I turn towards everything that surrounds me for guidance. And probably most of all, I turn *within*.

## Reflection Questions:

- How did you feel throughout this moon cycle?
- Did connecting with the moon feel natural, or did it feel awkward at times?
- Did you ever feel "silly" or self-conscious while doing the rituals? What did that bring up for you?
- Were there moments of clarity, inspiration, or heightened energy you can link to a particular phase of the moon?
- Did any synchronicities or "small miracles" happen that felt connected to your intentions?
- What surprised you most about this experience?

## Further Reading & Inspiration:

- **"Moonology"** by Yasmin Boland
- Look up Mary Oliver's poem "Moon and Water"
- The "Deluxe Moon" app (for tracking phases)

Your space for notes, doodles & drawings:

## Women Wild

We are the ones with the laughter in our voices
and the mud between our toes, the ones who elevate a sister
rather than frowning at her stories.

We are the ones with the sun-kissed cheeks
and the messy, salty hair, the ones who sing to whales
and smell the change of seasons in the air.

We are the ones with the hopes and dreams
lighting up our way, the ones who dance under the moon
and prepare for the new day

When our roar is loud enough to echo
through the world with might, and wild women everywhere hold
hands, then step into the light.

# sound healing

## The secret world of sound and vibration

*"If you want to find the secrets of the universe, think in terms of energy, frequency, and vibration."*

Nikola Tesla

Tesla's words have always stuck with me, and at one point in my rewilding journey I decided to take them seriously. What happens if you look at life through the lens of sound and vibration? What shifts when you pay attention to the energy that hums beneath everything we do?

When I dedicated a month to this practice, my challenge was simple: to become conscious of the sounds that shape my days. The obvious ones and the subtle ones. The background hums I usually ignore, and the songs that carry me through. Because sound is everywhere. It travels through walls and water. It lingers in our bones. It changes our moods instantly, lifting us, soothing us, agitating us, or pulling us back into memory. And yet, for most of us, it goes unnoticed.

This practice was my invitation to rewild my ears, to re-sensitise myself to the soundscape I live in. Not through expensive workshops or instruments, but through small, daily acts of listening and creating. Tiny practices that cost nothing but attention. Because sound has the power to transform us and to remind us that we, too, are vibrating, resonating, living bodies in a living world.

And here's where vibration comes in: Energy is the invisible currency we are all trading, all the time. You've felt it before: walking into a room and sensing immediately that something was "off." Or meeting someone whose warmth and kindness seemed to literally radiate into every corner of the space. That's because *it did*. A close friend once told me their therapist had a habit of always opening the window after each session. "For a breath of fresh air," she explained. But also, because she believed the energy of the person before needed to be released – their vibe, their heaviness, their leftover resonance – so the room could start fresh for the next. I love that example, because it makes something usually invisible very tangible: energy accumulates, shifts, and moves, and we can choose to notice and work with it. On that note, I once saw this note on a welcome-mat at somebody's house, and I've remembered it ever since:

***"Please be responsible for the energy you bring into our home."***

What you can expect from this practice is not a course in music, nor a study in acoustics or physics, but a chance to listen differently. To notice the sounds that hold you, whether you live in a quiet village, a city street, or an apartment with thin walls. To play with vibration in your own body through voice, breath, or instruments and see how it shifts your energy.

When I gave myself this focus for a month, I opened my window each morning to the sounds outside, sat on my porch with my coffee in complete stillness, picked up my guitar again after years of neglect, and rediscovered the hum of my own voice. And I discovered that, when you make space for sound, it begins to answer back. The forest, the street, the wind, even your own body, all of them vibrate, all of them communicate. And you realise you're part of a much larger choir. Once you've noticed it, you can't un-hear it.

## Embracing sound & vibration in daily life

One of the first things I noticed when I dedicated a month to sound was how much of it I normally tune out. There is no shortage of sound in our lives – cars outside, voices in the next room, phones buzzing, music streaming from every café. And yet, for all this noise, we often don't truly *hear*. We become deaf to the subtle textures, and especially the natural rhythms, the invisible flow of vibration around us.

This deafness isn't accidental. Modern life pushes us toward distraction and disconnection. We fill silences with podcasts and playlists; we shut out background noise with headphones. And yet, sound is never absent. Even when we think we're in silence, there is always something humming, vibrating, resonating. When we ignore it, we miss the chance to participate in that deeper rhythm.

Rewilding my awareness of sound meant making space for listening again. Noticing how rain on the roof has a rhythm of its own. How my footsteps sound different on wet leaves versus dry soil. How birds in the morning carry a different melody than at dusk. These details were always there; I had simply stopped paying attention. Once I did, everything felt more alive.

It also made me more aware of the sounds I create myself. The music I choose, the words I speak, even the thoughts I repeat in my head. All of them have vibration, and they shape the atmosphere around me. It's easy to forget this, to think sound is something happening "out there." But sound begins inside us, too. My voice, my breath, my hum… these are also vibrations, and they affect not only me but the people around me, and much more than we think.

## Practical ways to welcome sound and vibration

When I set out to explore sound, I started with small shifts. Things anyone can do, most of them free. And yet, those small shifts made the biggest difference. Here are the practices I explored during my sound month, and the ones you might like to try yourself.

### Open the window.

Each morning, the very first thing I did was let the outside in. Sometimes it was birdsong, sometimes rain on the leaves, sometimes only the hum of a busy street. It didn't matter. What mattered was noticing: This is the sound of the world I wake into today. Try it tomorrow morning. Open the window before you look at your phone. Stand there for a minute, listening. Ask yourself: what kind of energy does this sound carry? How does it make me feel?

### Wake and sleep with sound.

I swapped my phone alarm for a small nightlight clock with nature sounds. At night, I fell asleep to ocean waves. In the morning, I woke to bird calls. These tiny bookends to the day changed more than I expected. And because my phone no longer lived on my nightstand, I found myself reading again at night instead of scrolling. You don't need to buy a new gadget like I did. If you're comfortable with your phone in the bedroom, you can set up free playlists on your phone, or find recordings of waves, rain, or forest sounds. Experiment: what sound relaxes you into sleep? What sound lifts you gently into the morning?

### Play an instrument, even badly.

I picked up my guitar again, an old companion since I was thirteen, and committed to playing a little every day. Just a few songs. One new tune each week. My fingers hurt at first, then toughened. My energy lifted. Making sound myself, rather than only consuming it, filled me in a way I had forgotten.

Do you have an instrument tucked away somewhere? A guitar, a keyboard, a ukulele? Dust it off. Play something simple. Don't worry how it sounds. Or, if no instrument is at hand, try singing. Hum along to a song you love. Let your own sound vibrate through your body.

**Sit in stillness.**

Every morning, I took my tea or coffee onto the porch, closed my eyes, and listened. Nothing else. Thoughts, birds, wind, feelings, all of it. Sometimes I wrote a question in my journal. Sometimes I spoke a few words aloud, like a conversation with the universe. I'm sure I looked odd to anyone passing by, but those moments became precious. They taught me that silence is never silent.
Take your drink outside tomorrow or sit by an open window. Close your eyes. What do you hear when you stop trying to control the moment?

**Use what you already have.**

For years, a small sound bowl sat on my desk gathering dust. During this monthly practice I finally began to use it. The tone was wobbly at first, then steadier. I liked having it within reach while I worked, a reminder to pause and reset the energy in the room. Look around your own space. Do you own something that makes sound – a bowl or an old bell? Bring it into your daily rhythm. Let it call you back to presence.

**Curate the soundtrack of your day.**

Pay attention to the music in your life. Does it support your energy, or drain it? Experiment: try working in silence, with instrumental music, with voices, or with devotional chants like Kirtan. Notice how each changes your focus, your mood, your creativity. I like to start the day with a super-positive and playlist (and might even dance a little if the mood strikes me). This sets me up for a good day.

**Sing or hum into your body.**

One of the simplest and most powerful ways to work with vibration is through your own voice. For me, singing has always been medicine. It shifts my mood faster than almost anything else, and it connects me instantly to my body. When

I began singing regularly again, even just a few minutes a day, I noticed my energy rise and my stress fall away. It doesn't matter if you're "good" at it. In fact, the less you care how you sound, the more freeing it becomes.

If singing feels daunting, try humming instead. Place one hand gently on your belly, and hum a long, steady tone. Feel the vibration travel into your palm. Keep humming until you notice something shift, a little softening, a little release. This simple practice is known to calm the nervous system. It quiets the mind because while you hum, intrusive thoughts can't push their way in. All that matters is the vibration moving through you.

In yogic tradition, this is taken a step further with the sacred syllable OM (or AUM). It is considered the sound of the Universe itself, the original vibration from which everything else arises. When you chant OM, you're aligning your own body with that universal frequency. Whether you see it as a spiritual truth or as a metaphor, the effect is the same: you feel connected, expanded, steadied. I've often used OM or a deep hum when I feel tightness in my chest or stress in my belly, and each time it feels like the sound melts the knots inside me.

**Try this:** close your eyes, inhale deeply, and as you exhale chant a long "OM." Notice how it vibrates first in your chest, then your throat, then your head. Repeat three times and see how you feel.

## Reflections on the practice

What surprised me most when I dedicated a month to sound was how little it took to feel a difference. Opening a window, humming into my belly, strumming a few chords on the guitar… these were small, free, ordinary acts. And yet they shifted so much. I felt calmer, happier, more awake and more alive.

It reminded me that the real challenge isn't money or equipment or time. The real challenge is consistency. These practices are simple but staying with them day after day is harder than it looks. That's part of why I created my rewilding year in the first place: to hold myself accountable, to make sure I didn't let the busyness of life sweep these things aside.

Working with sound also taught me something important about energy: it responds to resonance, not force. When something feels stuck, our instinct is often to push harder. But vibration works differently. Sometimes the most powerful shift comes not from effort, but from tuning yourself differently. Think of a radio: if the station is crackling, you don't yell at it, no, you adjust the dial. Life works the same way. When I changed the "frequency" – the music I played, the sounds I welcomed, the way I used my own voice – things around me began to shift, too.

This practice will open your ears, but it also opens something deeper: a sense that the world is humming all the time, and we are humming with it.

## Reflection Questions:
- What sounds stood out to you most during this practice?
- How does sound affect your mood or energy throughout the day?
- How did engaging with sound and vibration affect your sense of connection – to yourself, to others, to your surroundings?
- If you continue this practice, what would you like to explore more deeply?

## Further Reading & Inspiration:
- Playlists of nature sounds: streams of ocean waves, rain, forest, and birdsong you can listen to anytime. Just look for "Gisele Stein Author" on Spotify for my favourite playlists.
- Explore Kirtan music: both recorded and live. If you have the chance, attending a session in your area can be profoundly moving. There's nothing quite like chanting together in a group, feeling the vibration rise.
- The Healing Power of Sound by Mitchell L. Gaynor: a modern classic on sound healing and vibration in everyday life.
- The World Is Sound: Nada Brahma by Joachim-Ernst Berendt: a beautiful exploration of ancient wisdom and modern science on sound as the essence of existence.

**Your space for notes, doodles & drawings:**

# A Whisper Wild

A whisper wild carried on the wind,

A call that stirred something deep within

I followed its voice to this rugged place,

And felt my soul come alive with grace.

This wild coast became my home,

A place to breathe, a place to roam.

I found love in every rock and stream,

Living life as if in a dream.

Now I watch the seasons come and go,

Witness the ocean's ebb and flow.

And as I look back on the last years,

I see how the forest swallowed all my fears.

My heart forever beats with the calm rhythm

Of this earth that I hold dear

And I hope that when I leave this place,

A whisper wild will linger here.

# earthing

## Returning to the ground beneath your feet

Grounding, or earthing, is the practice of placing your body in direct contact with the Earth's surface so that you can reconnect with its natural electric charge. When your bare feet touch ground, or when you lie down on the forest floor, your body absorbs free electrons from the Earth. These tiny particles have a stabilising, calming effect on your nervous system and your overall health.

Or so the theory goes. Think of it this way: your body already knows how to respond to the sun. When sunlight touches your skin, vitamin D is created, which is a vital process for your wellbeing. The Earth, under your feet at every moment, offers its own form of nourishment. Its surface holds a steady current of energy and frequencies that quietly influence your body at a deep level, regulating, repairing, and reminding you of your natural rhythms.

Earthing isn't new. For most of their existence, humans (just like any other animal!) lived in direct contact with the soil. Walking barefoot, sleeping on the ground, working with their hands in fields. Shoes, concrete, and indoor lives have insulated many of us from that connection. When you make time to step outside and let your skin meet the Earth, you begin to restore that lost relationship.

This month's practice invites you to slow down and return to something beautifully simple: the ground beneath your feet. It's a way of remembering that your body is not separate from the Earth, but part of it, tuned to the same natural currents that flow through rivers, forests, and sky.

## Why earthing? – The health benefits

So why make the effort to practice earthing? The benefits are surprisingly wide-ranging, and many people notice subtle shifts almost immediately.

- **Reduced inflammation.** Chronic inflammation is at the root of so many modern illnesses. Studies suggest that direct contact with the Earth helps calm inflammation in the body, giving your cells a chance to recover and repair.
- **Pain relief.** Whether it's long-term aches or something more acute, earthing often eases discomfort. Many people who practice regularly speak of pain fading in ways that feel almost miraculous.
- **Stress relief.** One of the first changes you might notice is a sense of calm. Standing barefoot on the ground seems to send a message straight to the nervous system: you are safe. You can let go.
- **Improved circulation.** Research shows earthing helps the blood flow more freely, which may lower the risk of cardiovascular problems and leave you feeling lighter and more energised.
- **Better sleep.** This one matters to me personally. Many people (myself included) report drifting off more easily and sinking into deeper, more restorative sleep after regular grounding.
- **Vitality and energy.** With time, earthing often leads to a steady increase in energy, clarity, and a feeling of being alive in your own skin.

## How to do earthing

So how do you actually practice earthing? Well, there are two main ways to approach it.

### 1. Outdoor earthing

The most natural way is to step outside and let your skin meet the ground. Walk barefoot on grass, soil, sand, or even concrete. Sit under a tree with your back against the trunk, dig your hands into the soil while gardening, or lie down in a meadow and let the earth hold your weight.

What I love most about this form of earthing is its simplicity: it's free. A patch of grass in a city park, a stretch of sand by the sea, even a small garden bed can reconnect you in minutes. No equipment, no memberships, no barriers. All you need is the willingness to take off your shoes, slow down, and make contact.

### 2. Indoor earthing

During my research, I discovered something I hadn't realised before: grounding can also happen indoors. There are mats, blankets, and even bed sheets designed to connect with your home's electrical grounding system. These allow your body to access the Earth's charge while you sleep, work at your desk, or relax in the evening.

This can be a wonderful solution in winter, for those with limited mobility, or for anyone living in a place where daily outdoor contact isn't possible. I was curious enough to order a grounding mat myself, and I've even recommended it to a friend who deals with chronic pain. While nothing replaces the feeling of bare feet on living soil, these tools can extend the practice into everyday life and make it more consistent.

## Why I decided to try earthing

For me, earthing felt like the most natural next step in this rewilding year. When you think about it, every other animal on this planet walks barefoot. To me, it seemed as essential as drinking water or getting enough rest. If we're serious about rewilding ourselves, then reconnecting with the ground beneath us may be the single most important practice to integrate into daily life.

Beyond that bigger picture, I also had a few very personal reasons for giving earthing a try:

- Sleep: Like many people, I struggled with falling and staying asleep and wanted to explore a natural solution.
- Hormones: I'd been dealing with hormonal imbalances and was curious whether earthing might help regulate my system.
- Circulation: My blood tends to thicken easily, and my arms and legs often fall asleep quickly. Research suggested earthing could support better blood flow, which felt especially relevant for me.

## Restoring our lost connection

When I look at the way we live now, the disconnection from the ground beneath us seems obvious. Shoes with rubber soles, concrete floors, air-conditioned offices, and so much time spent indoors… we rarely, if ever, touch the Earth directly anymore. Somewhere along the way, we even began separating ourselves in language, referring to "nature" as though it's something outside of us. Lately I've preferred using the word Earth instead. That small shift reminds me that we are part of the whole, not separate from it. Earthing is one way to close that gap, to step back into a more natural state of being. It's not a new idea; our ancestors lived this way all the time. But for us it feels like rediscovery. A practice of remembering what the body already knows: how to belong to the Earth.

## The science behind earthing

Okay, now let's get a bit nerdy for a moment and talk about the science behind grounding. I am obviously not a scientist, so I'm going to keep this section brief, but I would suggest, you look up a couple of studies if you want to learn more. So, to keep it simple, it all comes down to two things: the electrical nature of the Earth and the electrical nature of our own bodies. And the Earth's surface basically has an endless supply of free electrons, thanks to the global atmospheric electrical circuit, and these electrons give the Earth a natural negative charge. Now, our bodies, being mostly water and minerals, are excellent conductors of electrons. And when we make direct contact with the Earth, there's a transfer of electrons from the Earth to our bodies. And it is this transfer that seems to have a bunch of beneficial effects:

- It neutralises free radicals: Free radicals are these positively charged molecules that can cause stress. The negative electrons from the Earth can neutralise these little troublemakers.
- It reduces inflammation: By neutralising those free radicals and affecting other processes, earthing has a significant anti-inflammatory effect.
- It affects the nervous system: Some research suggests that earthing can help regulate the nervous system, which promotes a shift from "fight or flight" mode to "rest and digest" mode.
- And lastly, it improves blood flow: Earthing has been shown to improve circulation and reduce cardiovascular risk.

So, in its essence, Earthing is Mother Nature's original anti-inflammatory solution. What's not to like? When you take your shoes off and place your feet on the earth, something subtle begins to shift. At first it may feel simple, even ordinary, but with time you start to notice how steadying it is, how your body responds in ways you didn't expect. The ground has always been there, quietly offering its support, waiting for you to remember.

This practice can be a powerful reminder that you belong here, fully and completely. You can step outside at any moment and reconnect, no special tools or rituals required. Allow yourself to lean into that connection, to feel the energy move through you, to know that you are part of a living, breathing planet. And once you've felt that sense of belonging, it becomes something you can return to whenever you need steadiness, calm, or a gentle reset.

## Reflection Questions:
- Did you notice any shifts in your energy, mood, or sleep after trying earthing?
- Were there moments of resistance? Discomfort, self-consciousness, distraction? What did those reveal to you?
- If you tried indoor earthing (mat, sheet, or blanket), how did the experience compare to being outside?
- How connected do you currently feel to the ground beneath you in daily life? Has this practice changed that awareness?
- In what ways might you bring more barefoot moments into your routine, small, everyday ways that feel doable?
- How does it feel to think of yourself as part of the earth, rather than separate from "nature"?

## Further Reading & Inspiration:
- Earthing: The Most Important Health Discovery Ever! by Clinton Ober, Stephen T. Sinatra, and Martin Zucker: the foundational book that sparked modern interest in the practice.
- The Earth Prescription by Laura Koniver, MD: a gentle guide with simple, practical ways to ground yourself daily.
- Online: Earthing Institute (earthinginstitute.net): a resource hub for research, FAQs, and product information.
- For inspiration: Try barefoot walking meditations, which combine mindfulness with grounding: many free recordings are available on meditation apps or YouTube.

Your space for notes, doodles & drawings:

# Small Nature

With slowness and with grace,
Nature moves at its own pace,
In ways that most won't even see,
Missing out on all its mystery.

The way the leaves of the trees
Sway gently in the breeze,
Or how the grasses bend and sway
As the wind carries them away.

The slow and steady growth
Of the lichens on the rock,
Or the way the flowers bloom
As if on nature's clock.

The way the spider weaves its web,
Or the snail that leaves a trail,
The movements may be small,
But they tell a bigger tale.

For nature is not in a rush,
It takes its time to unfold,
In ways that are so subtle,
Yet never do grow old.

And though we may not always see
The beauty in the slow,
It's there for all to cherish,
If we surrender to its flow.

So maybe take some time today
To pause and to appreciate
The slowness and the perfect grace
Of small nature, oh so great.

# speaking with nature

## Learning nature's language

There are moments in the wild when something feels... well, let's call it "slightly off." A bird tilts its ead, then moves closer when you ask him to. A horse leans in, mirroring your breath until you both stand still. A fox pauses on the path, watching you long enough for understanding to pass between you. Most of us dismiss these moments as coincidence. But what if they are part of a conversation we've forgotten how to have?

For most of human history, people lived in close relationship with animals, plants, and landscapes. Our survival depended on it. Hunters knew how to read the behaviour of birds to sense approaching predators. Gatherers learned to follow the rhythms of insects to find ripe fruit. Farmers watched the sky not only for weather but for subtle shifts in energy. This was their language: not words, but an exchange of signs, gestures, feelings, and vibrations.

Today, much of that sensitivity has gone quiet. We've been trained to value rational explanations over intuitive perception, to treat nature as scenery instead of kin. And yet, many people still report experiences of connection that defy logic: a sudden knowing, a feeling of being guided, a wordless recognition that passes between species. These moments suggest that communication with the more-than-human world may not be magic, but *memory*, a skill once common, still possible, waiting to be remembered.

It was with this in mind that I dedicated a month of my rewilding year to learning how to speak with nature.

Now, when I say communicating with animals or communicating with nature, I don't mean teaching your dog to sit or greeting your cat when you come home from work. Those things are real communication, of course. Your pet understands and responds, and anyone who has lived with animals knows how powerful body language and tone can be. But what I want to explore here is something even deeper.

Animal communicators sometimes describe it as telepathy: an invisible exchange of energy, images, or feelings between species. A silent network of communication that other beings seem to access naturally. If that sounds a little far-fetched to you, I understand. I'm not here to convince you. What I can share is what I've learned from research, from observation, and from dipping my toes into this mystery myself.

When I wrote my novel "The Age of Elephants", which features an animal communicator, I dove into this subject more deeply than ever before. I read books, watched documentaries, and spoke with people who dedicate their lives to this practice. I've also seen things in nature that I couldn't explain in any other way. Taken together, these experiences led me to believe that there is another kind of communication at play, even if I can't always access it myself.

I should say this upfront: I'm not one of the "gifted" ones. I didn't grow up with pets. Apart from a few fish in an aquarium, I didn't share my childhood with animals. For most of my life, I was – as I suspect many of us are – almost deaf to the deeper "song" of nature. I loved being outdoors, but I didn't know there was another way of listening.

My curiosity only really awakened when I trained as a safari guide in South Africa. Immersed in wild landscapes and close encounters with animals, I began to sense that something else was happening, just beneath the surface of what we call "observation." I couldn't name it then, but it stayed with me. And later, when I returned home, it became the seed for both my writing and my rewilding experiments.

I want to stress this: while I don't consider myself an animal communicator, everything I've read and heard suggests that this capacity lies dormant in all of us. Some may develop it more easily than others, but it is a skill that can be practiced, a sensitivity that can be reawakened. And in an age where our disconnection from the natural world is one of our greatest wounds, I believe it is worth exploring, not only for our own sake, but for the sake of the earth itself.

## Encounters on safari in South Africa

Although I've never experienced what animal communicators describe as clear telepathic connection, there have been moments in the wild when I felt something pass between myself and another being. And it might well be that the logical part of my mind is getting in the way here, talking down on experiences that might well have been much more special than I gave them credit for. But a few encounters from my time on safari have stayed with me like luminous threads woven into my memory:

### The elephant who wanted me to feel safe

For a season, my husband Frank and I guided safaris in Zambia. In one particular park, elephants were wary and quick to charge. The tragic result of relentless poaching and trophy hunting. Hunters often fired from vehicles, so elephants had learned to associate the sound of an engine with danger. There, we learned to keep our distance, driving on the moment we saw them, not daring to linger. It was the right thing to do. The fear etched into those animals was undeniable. When we returned to South Africa, still carrying that tension in our bodies, we met elephants again in the Greater Kruger National Park. One day, a female appeared with her calves, emerging from the bush to cross the road right in front of us. My heart pounded. Frank and I braced ourselves, convinced she would turn defensive at any moment. But once the young ones were safely across, she lingered for no apparent reason.

She turned toward us and stood very still, her gaze steady, calm and unhurried. Time seemed to stretch. I felt a shiver rise through me, goosebumps lifting my skin. It was as if she was saying: It's all right. You are safe here. We are safe. And in that quiet, suspended moment, I felt more clearly than ever that communication can happen beyond words. An endangered being, so vulnerable to human violence, seemed to reach across the gulf of species to reassure me.
A similar experience occurred with one of the oldest elephants bulls roaming the Kruger National Park at the time. "Proud", a researcher had named him.
One evening, as the last super full moon of the year was rising behind him, Proud approached our vehicle and lingered for an astoundingly long time *right* next to us. I swear, he was so close I could have reached out a hand and stroke his trunk. The encounter lasted for at least half an hour, with both Frank and my heart pounding as this giant just… stood there. It was quite nerve-wracking, actually. But I also remember a distinct feeling of frustration and disappointment on my part because I could not for the life of me decipher what he wanted. But he was incredibly peaceful and calm, swaying his head ever so gently, breathing the same

air as is. I will never forget that moment, suspended in time. Nor will I forget the day – it was maybe about a week or two later – when I read the news that Proud had passed away only the day before. And the question of what he was trying to say to us that night will probably stay with me forever, too.

**A sad, old leopard reaching out**
Another time, it was a leopard. We knew her well; she had held a territory near our family's vacation home for years. By then, she was growing old, her body leaner, her movements slower. For months she disappeared, and then one morning, she appeared again.

She approached us in a way she never had before. Normally she kept her distance, wild and self-possessed. That day she walked toward the vehicle, her eyes heavy with something that felt like sorrow. She made low, plaintive sounds, and when she looked at me, it felt like she was searching for recognition.

Of course, we couldn't intervene. She wasn't visibly injured, and the laws of the bush are clear: wild animals must remain wild. Still, the encounter unsettled me. A powerful predator, one I had always admired from afar, walked closer than ever before. Close enough that we had to move the car back to remain in our own comfort zone. And then, just as suddenly as she appeared, she was gone. That was the last time I saw her.

I don't know what it meant. Perhaps nothing. But it felt significant, as though she had chosen, in her final days, to be seen. To reach out across the divide, not in need, but in some mysterious form of communication that still resists explanation.

## How animal communicators work

The encounters I just shared were meaningful to me, but they're not proof of anything, of course. They don't prove that a deeper language exists between humans and animals. And that's part of why I wanted to learn more from those who dedicate their lives to this kind of work.

One name came up again and again in my research: Anna Breytenbach, a South African animal communicator whose work has reached people all over the world. I've never met her, but I've watched documentaries and interviews that left me deeply moved. One, in particular, has stayed with me.

In the film, a sceptical journalist sets out to test Anna. She wants to know if Anna's gift is real, so she follows her as she meets different animals she has never encountered before. The journalist watches, asks questions, and records what unfolds. It is fascinating to witness, because you can feel the journalist's doubt colliding with the possibility that something extraordinary is happening.

### How the black leopard "Diabolo" became Spirit

At the heart of the documentary is a black leopard, rescued and brought to a game farm in South Africa. His name was Diabolo, and he lived up to it. He was perpetually aggressive, unpredictable, impossible to approach. The caretakers did their best, but he remained hostile, pacing his enclosure with a rage no one could soothe.

When Anna met him, she didn't use force, or food, or training. She simply opened herself to him. And what she received was startling in its simplicity:

Diabolo let her know that he felt unseen. None of the humans in his life had ever acknowledged his dignity, his spirit. He wanted recognition. He wanted respect. And most of all, he wanted a new name.

So, they gave him one. From that day forward, Diabolo became Spirit. The transformation was visible almost immediately. He grew calmer, more approachable, more at peace. His caretakers were astonished. Watching the footage, I found myself astonished, too. Something in the leopard's eyes shifted. It was as if a weight had been lifted, not only from him, but from the space around him.

It is easy to dismiss stories like this, to reduce them to wishful thinking or clever training. But when you see the change with your own eyes, when you feel it in your own chest as you watch, it becomes harder to explain away. To me, Spirit's story is a reminder of what becomes possible when we dare to treat other beings as conscious, feeling, and dignified. When we speak to them as if they can answer. Because… they can. And they do.

## How I went about this

The first step for my Speaking-with-Nature-month was to create a daily rhythm. Each morning, before anything else, I went outside to sit on the terrace. I tried to meditate, though I'll admit meditation doesn't come easily to me. My mind is always full of characters and conversations from the stories I'm writing. Often, the moment I found stillness, new ideas would surge up and I'd have to grab a pen before they slipped away. Maybe this is why I'll never become a true animal communicator – the pull of words is always so strong. But I wanted to learn, to try, to see what might happen in the spaces between thoughts. And then something unexpected happened: The first one to reach out to me wasn't an animal at all, but a plant.

### The palm on the terrace

There on the terrace sat a potted palm I had half-forgotten. She'd been struggling for months, dropping fronds no matter how much I watered her. A strange yellow fungus had begun to sprout in her soil, so I'd moved her outside "for now" and then, if I'm honest, stopped paying much attention.

That morning, as I sat waiting for birds or kangaroos, it came to me with startling clarity: How can I hope to communicate with anything, while ignoring the life right in front of me?

It wasn't a voice, exactly, but it felt different from my own narration, different from the way I imagine things when I write. A nudge. A hunch. A thought that felt like it wasn't mine. And in that moment, I realised my first lesson: **before reaching for the extraordinary, I needed to tend to the ordinary.** Before longing for mystical encounters, I had to notice what was already present.

So, I repotted the palm. I trimmed away the dead branch, watered her deeply, and kept her close. Slowly, she began to recover. The fungus didn't return. And I began to feel that we had repaired something together. Not only her health, but my awareness.

We often ignore the things right in front of us. That potted palm taught me that speaking with nature doesn't begin with great visions or dramatic encounters. It begins with presence. With care. With noticing what we've overlooked.

**The importance of empathy**

The next shift came when I realised that sitting up on the terrace, a few steps removed from the earth, kept me apart. Communication, I was learning, is rooted in empathy: placing yourself in another's paws, hooves, or roots. So, I climbed down. I took off my shoes and pressed my bare feet to the ground. I leaned against the trunk of a tree. I let myself belong to the same level as everything else. If you try this yourself, I recommend choosing one place in nature that you return to again and again. It doesn't have to be grand, a bench in a city park, a corner of woodland, even a balcony with a single pot of green. Visit the same place regularly. Let your body grow familiar with it. Notice the subtle changes. The more you return, the easier it becomes to quiet yourself enough to listen.

**Your intention will make it happen**
What surprised me most during was this: once I had voiced my intention, once I had made the effort and claimed this as a practice, animals began to show up. Once I set the intention to communicate with nature, encounters began to unfold in ways that felt… uncanny. Animals are always around where I live, but I kid you not: during my month of animal communication, they appeared with a timing and frequency that felt charged, as if the world was listening.
First came the mouse. On the very week I declared this challenge, a small brown mouse slipped into the house. What are the chances? To be fair, I didn't exactly manage it gracefully – there was more chaos than conversation – but the symbolism wasn't lost on me. The invitation had been sent, and the response was immediate.
Then a sparrow. One morning it flew straight into the window and dropped onto a branch outside, dazed. I rushed to see if it was hurt. For a moment it clung to the branch, spinning in a strange little circle as though dizzy. I sat quietly beside it, whispering calm, letting it know I was there. Whether it understood me or not, I can't say, but after a while it steadied itself and flew off. That, too, felt like a reply.
And then came the dolphins.

**A special dolphin encounter**
On weekends, Frank and I often take our paddleboards into a nearby river. One morning, as we turned into a narrow, quiet stream, Frank asked offhandedly, "Do you think dolphins ever come up here?" I laughed and said I hoped so. Not sixty seconds later, the water ahead erupted in silver splashes. At first, I thought it was fish – until I saw them: four dolphins and a calf, swimming straight toward us!
I gasped so hard I covered my face with both hands. Goosebumps rose over my arms as the pod drew near. They dove beneath our boards and surfaced again in the channel beyond, sleek shadows gliding through the current. (I cannot emphasise this enough: this *never* happens!) We turned and followed them for a

while, our paddles barely breaking the water. It felt like such a blessing, and I was well aware that this was happening during my nature-communication-month. This was, as they say, my time to shine.

But in my excitement, I reached for them clumsily, chattering in my head like an over-eager child. *I'm here! I'm here! I'm so excited to see you!* It was pure joy but also overwhelming. Later I realised my mistake. Reaching out to an animal for the first time is like approaching a stranger on the street – you wouldn't run up shouting your delight. You'd be gentle, respectful, careful. In that first moment, I forgot. The dolphins rushed off, disappearing in the distance.

An hour later, however, as if to give me a second chance, they returned. After our paddle, I was going for a dip near the shore when I saw them again: the same five, including the calf, gliding upriver in perfect formation, coming straight towards me once again. This time I stayed still. I breathed slowly. I let the moment speak for itself. And they passed close, close enough that the water around me trembled with their movement. It was quiet, and it was perfect.

Twice in one day. A gift, and a lesson…

## A surprising lesson

….and that lesson is twofold: The first is that all of my encounters during that month might seem small, perhaps even insignificant to someone who wasn't there. But what I've come to realise is that this is how the Universe speaks. It speaks in quiet moments; in subtleties we often overlook. The more we pay attention, the more we allow these connections to happen, the more significant they become. Life feels richer. And in a way I can't quite explain, I believe nature is enriched, too. There is a give and take in this exchange, a mutual recognition, and it is a beautiful thing.

The second part is something I once heard phrased like this: when you ask the Universe for courage, it doesn't hand you courage. It gives you **the opportunity to be courageous.** In this context, that means when you set the intention for something – like communicating with nature – you don't get the result delivered to you ready-made. Instead, you are given openings, chances to practice, moments that invite you to take the step yourself. That is what I noticed during these weeks. The moment I voiced my desire to connect, animals began appearing in ways that caught my attention. It was still up to me to meet them halfway. And that, I think, is why this practice feels so meaningful: because it requires participation. It's not passive. It's a collaboration.

I'll continue with this work because it makes life feel fuller and because it reminds me that another story is possible in this world – one of connection, of reciprocity, of respect. And that, to me, brings hope. This lesson doesn't only apply to speaking with nature. It can shape every part of life. When you ask for something, don't wait for it to arrive wrapped and complete. Look for the opportunities you are given to bring it into being yourself. Step into them. That's when the magic unfolds.

## Speaking with Nature: a step-by-step guide for beginners

Here are the first steps that helped me begin, so you can explore this practice yourself this month:

### 1. Establish the connection.
Begin by becoming quiet. Put your phone away, step away from distractions, and give yourself extended time outdoors. Sit with your bare feet on the earth, lean against a tree, and simply listen. Let yourself feel the ground beneath you, the air around you, the presence of everything alive nearby.

### 2. Understand how messages arrive.
Nature rarely speaks in words. Instead, communication often comes as a feeling, a sudden image, or even a sensation in your body that mirrors what another might be experiencing. This is why time and practice matter: you need to grow attuned to your inner signals so you can begin to sense what is imagination and what might be genuine contact.

**3. Actively observe.**
Pay close attention to the being you want to connect with. Watch how it moves, how it rests, how it responds to its environment. The more familiar you become, the more easily you'll recognize when something unusual or meaningful occurs. With pets, this comes naturally because we already know their patterns. With wild animals, it takes patience and repetition. Each individual has its own quirks, and part of the work is learning to see them.

**4. Practice empathy.**
Try stepping into their world. What does this creature eat, where does it sleep, how does it spend its days? Reading and learning can help, but the heart of it lies in imagination and curiosity. The more you can see through their perspective, the deeper the sense of connection becomes.

**5. Learn to reach out.**
When you begin to communicate, approach with respect. Excitement is natural (I learned this the hard way with the dolphins) but the first contact is delicate. Step back, breathe, and ask simple questions: What should I call you? How do you feel? Is there something you'd like to share? Whether with a tree, a plant, or an animal, let it be an invitation, not a demand.

I have practiced this with my own plants, including the palm on the terrace that nearly gave up before I began listening. My great-grandmother did the same, speaking to her garden flowers each morning.
It may sound unusual to you, even a little unbelievable. But what I've found is this: **the moment I allowed for magic, magic appeared everywhere.** The act of listening, of treating the living world as kin, makes my days more vivid, more beautiful. And I can't help but wonder how different our world might feel if more of us tried.

For me, that is reason enough.

## Reflection Questions:
- Have you ever felt that a plant, tree, or animal was reaching out to you in some way? What happened?
- What small encounters (a bird at the window, a breeze, an unexpected animal sighting) might carry meaning if you paid closer attention?
- How do you usually react to these moments? Do you dismiss them, or allow them to matter?
- Where in your daily life could you create more space for noticing and listening?
- What would practicing empathy with another species look like to you? Can you imagine stepping into their paws, wings, or roots?
- Do you feel resistance to the idea of speaking with nature? If so, what part of you is resisting, and what might that resistance be trying to teach?

## Further Reading & Inspiration:
- Sandra Ingerman & Lynn Roberts: Speaking with Nature (The book that inspired this practice for me. A grounded, practical guide to listening more deeply to the living world)
- Look for Anna Breytenbach & the Black Leopard "Diabolo" on YouTube
- Social media & online communities: If you're curious, there are many animal communicators sharing their experiences online. Follow a few accounts that resonate with you

**Your space for notes, doodles & drawings:**

# The wild woman archetype

There are stories that surface across cultures, across centuries, carrying the trace of a figure both feared and revered. In the deserts of Mexico, she appears as La Loba, the wolf woman, who gathers bones and sings forgotten creatures back to life. In the forests of Greece, she is Artemis, running barefoot with her bow, companion to wild animals and protector of women. In Slavic folklore she takes the form of Baba Yaga, dwelling in her hut that stands on chicken legs, feared for her fierceness but sought out for her uncompromising wisdom.

These stories may seem far apart, but together they sketch the outline of something older: a presence women have always known. She is the part that will not be tamed, the one who remembers how to listen to the earth, who moves to the rhythm of moon and season, who refuses to forget her belonging to the wild. For generations, this aspect of womanhood was woven into daily life. She was the midwife, the healer, the one who read the skies and the turning of the soil. Her knowledge was not written down in books but passed hand to hand, body to body, season to season. And though the world has tried to quiet her – through suspicion, through dismissal, through fear – she has not disappeared. She waits in the marrow, in dreams, in the sudden urge to stand barefoot in the grass or to howl at the moon.

When we begin to pay attention to her, the world no longer feels like a straight line we must march along, but more like a circle, an ebb and flow. We notice when the body asks for stillness, when energy rises again, when it is time to speak, to act, to create, and when it is time to retreat, to release, to let go.

This is where the Wild Woman meets the cycles of the female body. The pulse of our hormones, the rhythm of bleeding and renewal, is not random. It is one of the oldest mirrors of the natural world, written into our very flesh. When we ignore it, life might feel like more of a struggle against the tide. When we learn to follow it, we begin to sense the same intelligence that guides rivers, seasons, and moonlight, and we realise that the Wild Woman has been here all along, asking us to remember. For many of us, she has been silenced. Our culture prizes the hustle the endless productivity, not ebb and flow. Yet the Wild Woman never vanishes. She waits deep within our bones, ready to remind us of what we already know: we are cyclical beings.

## The wild rhythm of your body

One of the most profound ways the Wild Woman speaks is through the female cycle. For too long, menstruation has been treated as an inconvenience, something to hide or push through. But when we look through the lens of the wild, we see something very different.

Your cycle is not a flaw. It is an ancient rhythm, as old as the moon, as precise as the tide. And each phase carries its own medicine:

- The menstrual phase is a cleansing, a natural release. Just as trees shed their leaves, the body lets go of what is no longer needed. In this quiet descent, there is wisdom. Dreams may feel stronger, intuition sharper. The veil between inner and outer is thin. It is a time to ask questions, to listen deeply, to allow space for what wants to be born once the blood has passed.

- The follicular phase (the days after bleeding) carries a rising energy, a fresh wind. This is the Wild Woman stretching after rest, curious, ready to play and create.
- Ovulation is the full bloom. Radiant, outward, magnetic. It is a time for connection, communication, and bringing visions into the world.
- The luteal phase brings a turning inward. Energy dips, irritations rise to the surface. But here too is medicine: the chance to see clearly what no longer aligns, to prune away the dead wood.

When you begin to see your cycle this way, it shifts from being a burden into becoming a guide. Instead of fighting against your body, you *move with it*. You start to notice when to rest, when to push forward, when to plan, when to release. Reconnecting with your cycle is one of the most direct ways to rewild yourself. It brings you back into relationship with the body's truth, instead of the expectations of a world that asks you to be the same every day.

The Wild Woman Archetype shows us that there is power in flux, beauty in bleeding, clarity in darkness. She reminds us that cycles are not weakness but wisdom. And when you begin to honour your own rhythms, something softens. You stop apologising for needing rest. You begin to trust your own timing. You realise that the menstrual phase is not the end of the road each month, but the soil out of which new beginnings will grow. To live this way is an act of remembering and rebellion. A return to what women once knew: that our bodies are not machines but living landscapes, as seasonal and sacred as the Earth.

# wild swimming

## You are water

*"Empty your mind, be formless, shapeless, like water. If you put water into a cup, it becomes the cup. You put water into a bottle, it becomes the bottle. You put it in a teapot, it becomes the teapot. water can flow or it can crash. Be water, my friend."*

- Bruce Lee

Water has a way of pulling us back to something ancient. To sink beneath the surface of a lake, river, or ocean is to remember, at least for a moment, that our bodies are mostly water, too. Many people turn to wild swimming for resilience, for healing, or simply for the thrill of feeling alive. It is one of the most direct, physical ways to rewild yourself. Cold water clears the mind, shocks the body awake, and reminds you that you are both fragile and strong at once.

For this practice, I want to give you something tangible to take away. During my own Rewilding Year, I dedicated four weeks to wild swimming, and something shifted for me in that time, not in the way I first imagined, but in a way that was even more meaningful.

## Why wild swimming?

When I sat down to map out my Rewilding Year, wild swimming leapt straight onto the list. I'd always been drawn to it, though if I'm honest, much of that came from what I'd seen online: icy lakes, brave swimmers breaking holes in the ice, Wim Hof devotees swearing by the magic of cold immersion. I imagined myself doing something similar… suffering nobly in freezing water, toughening body and spirit.

But that's not what happened. I acknowledged quickly that I am not someone who enjoys the cold, and I cannot bring myself to do so. I love warmth. I thrive in wool socks, steaming soups, and endless cups of tea, especially in the second half of my cycle when my body is most sensitive to the chill.

At first, I tried to push through. But the truth is, wild swimming, in the sense of forcing myself into icy water every single day, wasn't right for me. And a huge part of this Rewilding Year is listening to those truths. So, I gave myself permission not to swim daily. Instead, I honoured what my body needed. And in doing so, I discovered a version of wild swimming that was far less about discipline and far more about relationship.

## Why the Wim Hof method isn't for everyone

There is no denying the power of Wim Hof's work. His breathing techniques and ice immersions have helped thousands, and I have deep respect for that. But much of the research around cold-water-immersion, much of the hype, has been centred on men's bodies. Very little has been studied when it comes to women's cycles, hormones, and the ways cold exposure might affect us differently.

That gap matters. For me, forcing myself into icy water felt more punishing than liberating, and I knew I had to approach this practice differently. Following the example of women like Jonna Jinton (the Swedish artist and YouTuber who swims through holes cut in frozen lakes) can be deeply inspiring. But it doesn't mean *every body* is called to that path.

Wild swimming, as I've come to see it, doesn't have to be about endurance or suffering. It can be about joy, presence, and listening. It can be slipping into water on a bright day and feeling yourself dissolve into its embrace. It can be noticing how the same river feels utterly different in wind, in sunshine, in stillness. It can be meeting water not as an adversary, but as a companion.

## Honouring our soft, feminine side

During my wild swimming month, I discovered that it doesn't serve me to approach rewilding, or life for that matter, in the way media often prescribes, or in the way men have modelled it in the past. For me, wild swimming became a lesson in listening closely to what my body needs, and in honouring my softer, feminine side.

There is space for gentleness. We are not all the same. What energizes one body might exhaust another. And as women, we carry cycles and rhythms that call for different approaches at different times. Honouring those rhythms is not weakness; it is wisdom.

And this listening led me to notice other ways I was moving against myself. One of the most immediate changes was deleting Instagram from my phone. The endless scrolling, the dopamine hits, the fast-paced pressure of constant comparison… it all felt like the exact opposite of what my body and spirit were asking for. Letting go of it felt like exhaling after holding my breath for too long. I didn't set out on this challenge searching for answers, but water has a way of revealing what wants to be seen. By slowing down, by honouring softness instead of striving, I began to notice the quiet truths that were waiting just beneath the surface. And once again, another rewilding month turned into something entirely unexpected, providing me with lessons tailored exactly to me. That is why your Rewilding Year will not look like mine. What's waiting around your river bend will be entirely your own.

## The significance of water

Much of what I'm about to say may sound obvious at first. We all know we need water to survive. We drink it, we cook with it, we wash with it. Every living being depends on it. But beyond this practical necessity lies something deeper, a pull that is woven into our evolution and our instincts.

For most of human history, water has meant safety. A freshwater source promised not only hydration but also food and shelter. It's no wonder that standing at the edge of a lake or river still evokes a sense of ease. Somewhere inside us, an ancient part recognises water as security.

There's also the intimate truth of our own bodies: **we are, in essence, water.** Around sixty percent of the human body is liquid. Which means that when we immerse ourselves in a river, lake, or ocean, we are a body of water meeting another body of water. To float is to remember what we are made of. To swim is to return to belonging.

Perhaps this is why the sensation of weightlessness feels so profoundly good. Floating carries us back to our very first experience of life, nine months held in amniotic fluid, suspended in the womb. Before we even breathed air, we knew water. In that sense, every time we step into a river or the sea, we are returning to our first home.

This is why I believe rewilding cannot be complete without water. It covers seventy percent of the planet, and it makes up most of us. To reconnect with water is to reconnect with life.

## Beating procrastination with wild swimming

Something practical I'll carry into other parts of my life from now on is that the fear is always worse than the plunge. In the beginning, I wasted so much time standing on the edge, hesitating, bargaining with myself. By the end of my wild swimming month, I learned to simply jump. The anticipation was so much colder than the water itself. Once submerged, my body adjusted, my strokes carried me, and soon there was joy where only dread had been.

And that lesson belongs not only to swimming but to everything else I do, especially writing my books. Writing, for me, often begins with avoidance. I clean the kitchen, scroll through Instagram, answer emails, or find any excuse not to sit down at the page. It isn't laziness; it's fear. Fear of not being good enough, fear of what will (or won't) appear once the cursor blinks back at me. Staring at the blank page feels unbearable, until the first sentence lands. Then the next follows, and suddenly… I'm swimming.

And that's probably the truest thing I've learned this month:

**The current will hold you, but first, you have to jump in.**

## 10 ways to harness the healing power of water (even if you don't live by the ocean)

Not everyone lives by the sea or near a river. But water is everywhere. We drink it, bathe in it, cook with it, listen to it falling from the sky. You don't need a dramatic plunge into icy waves to connect with its healing power. Here are ten ways to let water support you in everyday life:

**1. Drink with awareness.** Start your day with a glass of warm water, plain, or maybe with a little lemon or ginger. Instead of gulping it down absentmindedly, imagine where it travels inside you. Notice how it flushes your system awake, hydrating brain and body after sleep. Let drinking become a meditation: this simple act is what keeps you alive.

**2. Meditate with water.** Sit by a lake, river, or even a bowl of water in your home. If you don't have access to the real thing, listen to recordings of rain or waves. Focus on your pulse, your breath, and remember that your body is itself a flowing river, more than half made of water.

**3. Make moon water.** On the night of a full moon, leave a glass of water outside to absorb lunar light. The next morning, drink it, water your plants, or use it in cooking. It's a simple way to weave together two elemental forces: moon and water.

**4. Cleanse as ritual.** Turn your shower, face washing, or even house cleaning into a conscious act of release. Imagine the water carrying away old energy, stale moods, and fatigue. When you scrub a dish or mop the floor, picture yourself inviting clarity and freshness back into your space.

**5. Gaze and give.** Find a body of water and spend time simply watching it. Let its ripples and reflections quiet your mind. If you feel moved, offer something safe and natural (a flower, a leaf, a piece of wood) with a silent wish or blessing, letting your intention float away.

**6. End with cold.** At the end of your shower, turn the dial to cold for just ten seconds. It's a small, fierce act that jolts you awake, strengthens immunity, and trains you to face discomfort head-on. It's also an excellent antidote to procrastination, proof that the hardest part is taking the plunge.

**7. Drink from copper.** Try storing your water in a copper bottle. Beyond the sustainability of reusing a vessel, many traditions believe copper "charges" the water with positive energy and even slows aging. Whether or not you believe the science, the act itself invites ritual back into the ordinary.

**8. Hug more.** Every hug is a meeting of two bodies of water. Research shows that especially women benefit from at least twenty hugs a day to reduce anxiety and regulate stress. If there's no one around, wrap your arms around yourself for a moment – it works too.

**9. Celebrate rain.** Next time it rains, resist the instinct to curse the weather. Step outside. Dance in puddles. Let raindrops hit your face. Then come back in, take a warm shower, and notice how alive you feel. Living off a rainwater tank has certainly taught me how precious each drop is.

**10. Give back to water.** We are bodies of water, and when oceans and rivers are polluted, we too are harmed. Protecting them is self-preservation. That might mean shorter showers, reusing cooking water for plants, or changing your diet to lower water use. However small, each act is a way of honouring the source that sustains us all.

## Reflection Questions:
- What does your body ask for when it comes to temperature, rhythm, or time in water?
- Where in your life do you hesitate at the edge of something, and what might it feel like to simply step in?
- Can you recall a moment when water felt like medicine, like it washed something away for you?
- How does your cycle, your energy, or your mood influence your relationship with water?
- If you don't have access to oceans or lakes, how might you create a daily or weekly ritual of connecting with water in other ways?

## Further Reading & Inspiration:
- Blue Mind by Wallace J. Nichols (A fascinating look at the science of why water so profoundly affects our brains, bodies, and moods)
- Why We Swim by Bonnie Tsui. (A lighter, story-rich exploration of our human love affair with swimming)
- Jonna Jinton's videos on YouTube (her icy swims in Swedish lakes are as haunting as they are inspiring)
- Explore Wim Hof's breathing and cold-water practices (even if you don't follow them fully, they spark ideas about resilience and the power of cold)

**Your space for notes, doodles & drawings:**

# The Path

A winding path before me lies,
A journey that is mine alone,
The woods are dark, the skies are wide,
And I must find my own way home.

Through tangled roots and rocky crags,
I forge ahead with fearless stride,
The courage in my heart, it flags,
But Nature's beauty is my guide.

The wind that whispers in the trees,
It tells me secrets, mysteries,
Of paths not taken, lives unled,
And all the wonders still ahead.

The sun that shines upon my face,
It warms me with its gentle grace,
And fills my heart with hope and light,
To guide me through the darkest night.

And in the streams that rush and flow,
I find the strength to let it all go,
The doubts, the fears that hold me back,
And forge ahead on my own track.

Oh, let me walk this path with grace,
And find within this wild embrace,
The courage to be true and free,
And tread my own path fearlessly.

# crafting remedies

## Your own herbal apothecary

Imagine reaching for a jar you filled yourself, dried leaves you gathered under the sun, an oil you infused on your windowsill, a tincture you stirred with your own hands. Our ancestors lived this way, guided by knowledge passed through generations, rooted in trust that the land provides what we need. For most of human history, healing was brewed in kitchens, carried in pockets, whispered in recipes written by hand or held in memory – not bought, bottled up, in a pharmacy.

Working with herbs is rewilding because it pulls us back into that lineage. It places you in the role of healer, caretaker, creator. When you crush a sprig of rosemary, when you steep chamomile blossoms, when you pour honey over thyme, you are weaving yourself back into the long thread of relationship between people and plants, and you're gaining a sense of self-reliance that's an actual superpower in today's world.

This practice begins with attention and curiosity: noticing the plants around you, learning what they can offer, and daring to experiment. Each jar, bottle, or salve is a small rebellion against forgetting. It's a power flex in the truest sense: knowing how to soothe a burn, ease a cough, or calm your own nerves with what nature provides places you firmly in your own strength.

You don't need a wild meadow at your doorstep to begin. A windowsill herb, a pot of mint, or a bag of dried nettle from a local shop can become your entry point. What matters is that you place your own hands in the process. Crafting remedies awakens something ancient within you, something that remembers what it means to be both nurtured and empowered by the living world.

## Starting your own herbal apothecary

Of all the practices in this book, this one might ask you to spend some money at the beginning. Think of it as an investment in yourself. Once you've gathered a few tools and ingredients, you'll notice how quickly they pay you back. Instead of reaching for store-bought tea, lotion, or household cleaner, you'll have what you need to make your own. Little by little, the shelves in your home begin to look different: jars of herbs you dried yourself, bottles of golden oil infused with plants you love, salves that smell of beeswax and pine. Each item is both practical and personal, something you made with your own hands.

You don't need a full workshop to begin. A few simple tools are enough to get started:

- Pestle and mortar – to grind herbs, resins, or seeds.
- Strainer or sieve – to separate plant matter from liquid when making teas or infusions.
- Simmering pot – stainless steel or enamel is best, so nothing reacts with the herbs.
- Glass jars – any size will do, start with what you already have.

With those basics, you can brew teas, make infused oils, and prepare simple remedies. From there, you can expand your collection as your confidence grows.

Many items can be improvised or repurposed from what you already own, while others are worth the investment because they make the work smoother and your preparations last longer.

Here are some of the most useful tools and ingredients to add as you go:
- Double boiler (or a heat-safe bowl over a pot) – for melting wax and combining oils gently.
- Digital scale, measuring cups, and spoons – for consistent recipes.
- Metal funnel – to pour liquids neatly into bottles.
- Labels and a marker – to track what you've made and when.
- Wooden spoon, glass or stainless-steel bowls – to stir, mix, and pour.
- Dropper bottles – perfect for tinctures (reusing empty skincare bottles works well).
- Spray bottles – for herbal spritzers or room cleansers.
- Beeswax or soy wax, shea butter, and olive oil – the building blocks of salves, lotions, and balms.
- Herb scissors or pruning shears – to harvest plants with care.
- Drying racks or screens – to preserve herbs for teas and remedies.
- Grater – useful for beeswax or harder ingredients.

Start with what you can, improvise and reuse where possible, and let your apothecary grow slowly. You'll find yourself reaching less for packaged goods and more for what you've created, and that feels not only empowering but deeply satisfying.

**Copy my approach:**
When I began exploring medicinal herbs and plants, I approached it as a curious student, willing to learn by doing. What I share here is not a finished path, but an unfolding one, and you are warmly invited to step into it alongside me.

This desire has been with me for a long time. I always wanted a place where jars of dried leaves and roots lined the shelves, where oils and salves waited in dark glass bottles, where medicine came from the land.

But for years my life was too transient for such a thing. I moved too often, never staying long enough to tend plants, sometimes not even long enough to own proper furniture. I lived like a nomad. Only now, after settling down, do I finally have the stability to create the kind of home where these witchy dreams can take root.

## So why begin an apothecary at all?

For me, it ties back to a larger vision Frank and I have carried for years: one day living fully off grid, with solar on the roof, water tanks at the back, a garden bursting with food, a couple of dogs at our feet. Recently, we took a big step toward that dream by buying a piece of land, though for now we are still renting the cabin we live in until we can afford to build. And yet, I've always believed that if you want to call something into your life, you start by embodying it in small ways right where you are. You show up as the woman you want to become, long before her life has fully arrived.

For me, that woman is kneeling in the soil with muddy hands and a straw hat, harvesting tomatoes she grew herself. She knows how to make her own medicine, to live in harmony with the earth, and to care for herself and those she loves with remedies she crafted. Beginning an apothecary is my way of stepping into her shoes, even now, on a smaller scale.

Interestingly, what finally pushed me into action was my writing. One of the characters in my current witchy fantasy novel is an herbalist with her own apothecary, and research gave me the perfect excuse to dive in. But very quickly it turned into a chain reaction, one small choice pulling on a hundred others, in how I shop, what I make, what I bring into my home. I think I always sensed it would be like this, which is probably why I put it off for so long. I knew once I began, everything else would shift with it.

And it has.

## The life-changing art of working with herbs

As soon as you begin exploring how to make your own skincare, cleaning products, or even food with herbs, the process reaches further, it asks you to prepare, to slow down, to consider each step with care.

Before mixing oils or melting wax, you find yourself cleansing your workspace and making sure your tools are clean. You notice where your ingredients come from and whether they carry the same integrity you want to infuse into your remedies. Once your balm is complete, you place it on your bathroom shelf, and suddenly you want that shelf to be cleared, the room fresh, the whole home lightened and renewed... **Working with herbs ripples outward. It touches everything you do.** That's part of what makes this practice so transformative.

When I began, I read widely and collected ideas. Some herbalists suggest starting small: spend a full moon cycle with a single plant. Watch it, taste it, note how it changes. Let it become familiar before moving on to another. Others offer lists of simple herbs that grow easily in pots or windowsills. I followed some of this advice and ignored other parts. Mostly, I trusted my intuition and leaned toward the plants that called to me.

## Don't be overwhelmed

Two cautions became clear very early on. First, the world of herbal remedies can feel overwhelming. There are countless plants, each with their own uses, personalities, and cautions. Add to that the allure of lunar timing, tools, and endless tutorials online, and it's easy to lose yourself in the abundance of information. Second, it can also tempt you into overspending. Rows of dried herbs, beeswax, oils, glass jars, copper funnels, all of it looks just so enchanting, doesn't it? And we need it all. But the truth is, you don't need much to begin, and you likely already own more than enough to start.

This practice doesn't require you to overhaul your entire household overnight. It's fine to keep your supermarket shampoo or drink from tea bags while you experiment with making your own. Every small step counts, and each one brings a sense of achievement. Begin where you are, with what you have. From there, you can slowly build your own rhythm, your own apothecary, your own way of weaving herbs into daily life.

## What plants to start with?

The beginner plants I decided I wanted fresh in my house are:

- **Basil:** Basil is used to help with stomach problems and to fight germs. It's also made into oils to ease headaches and calm nerves.
- **Rosemary:** Rosemary is used to improve memory and boost brain power. It's made into creams to help sore muscles and joint pain.
- **Lemon Balm:** Lemon balm is used to help people relax and sleep better. Can be made into teas to ease stomach upset and stress.
- **Mint:** Mint is used to help with breathing problems and to cool down fevers. Can be put into oils to ease headaches and clear stuffy noses.
- **Aloe Vera:** Aloe vera is used on the skin to help burns, cuts, and rashes heal faster. Can be mixed into drinks to help with digestion and clean out the gut.
- **Chamomile:** Chamomile is used to calm people down and help them sleep. It's also made into creams to soothe itchy skin and help with eczema.

Then I also bought some dried herbs, although in the future I will start growing these myself as well:

- Lavender
- More chamomile
- Nettle
- Pine
- Cinnamon

Now, the next question I asked myself was, what is it that I would like to make?

And you might ask: Well, what *can* I make? The list is, of course, endless. But just to give you some ideas:

- Teas and infusions
- Tinctures (herb extracts in alcohol)
- Salves and balms
- Herbal oils
- Syrups
- Compresses
- Herbal bath blends
- Herbal sachets or pillows
- Herbal honeys
- Essential oils (through distillation)
- Lip balms
- Soaps
- Laundry Liquid
- Kitchen Cleaner
- Bathroom Cleaner
- Smudge Sticks
- And so much more…

During my "crafting remedies" month, I decided to make:

- Herbal Sachets to put under our pillows
- Kitchen Cleaner
- A Bath Blend
- And a Calming Hand Balm

Each of these took only a couple of minutes to make; the longest (and the most fun) one was the Calm Balm which took about half an hour. On the following pages, you can find the step-by-step recipes for each.

## Four easy-peasy recipes to take your first steps in your herbal apothecary:

*(Before making the following, I'd suggest cleaning your workspace and calming yourself. Then, once you get going, think about the intention you'd like to infuse each recipe with)*

### How to make your own calm balm:

### Materials:
- About ½ to 1 cup of your chosen dried herbs (I'm using lavender and chamomile)
- 2 cups of olive oil
- About 1 cup of beeswax or soy wax
- Double boiler
- Stirring utensil
- Strainer
- Glass jars (preferably short with wide openings for easy access)

### Instructions:
1. Infuse the oil: Gently heat the olive oil and dried herbs in the top of a double boiler over simmering water for about 15 minutes.
2. Strain the mixture: Pour the infused oil through a strainer into a small bowl, discarding the herbs. Return the strained oil to the double boiler.
3. Add essential oil: If desired, add a few drops of essential oil for extra fragrance. I'm using lavender oil to complement the herbs, but you can choose any scent you like.
4. Melt the coconut butter: Add the beeswax/ soy wax to the infused oil and heat gently until it's completely melted and incorporated.
5. Check consistency: Place a small amount on a spoon and allowing it to cool. If it's too soft, add more wax; if too firm, add more olive oil.
6. Pour and set: Once you're happy with the consistency, pour the warm balm into clean glass jars. Let it cool and solidify completely before capping the jars.

**How to make your own kitchen cleaner:**

**Materials:**
- 1 cup white vinegar
- 1 tablespoon dishwashing liquid
- 10-15 drops pine essential oil
- 2 cups water
- 16 oz spray bottle
- Funnel (optional, but helpful)

**Steps:**
- Pour 1 cup of white vinegar into the spray bottle. Use a funnel if needed to avoid spills.
- Add 1 tablespoon of dishwashing liquid to the vinegar.
- Carefully add 10-15 drops of pine essential oil. Adjust the amount based on your scent preference.
- Fill the rest of the bottle with 2 cups of water, leaving a little space at the top for shaking.
- Securely attach the spray nozzle to the bottle.
- Gently shake the bottle to mix all ingredients thoroughly.
- Label your bottle with the contents and date of creation.

To use: Shake well before each use. Spray on kitchen surfaces and wipe clean with a cloth or sponge.

Note: Always test on a small, inconspicuous area first to ensure compatibility with your surfaces. This cleaner is not recommended for use on marble or natural stone surfaces due to the acidic nature of vinegar.

**How to make your own herbal sachets to put under your pillow for better sleep:**

**Materials:**
- Small fabric pouches or squares of fabric (cotton or muslin work well; I used plant-based cleaning cloths I still had at home)
- Dried herbs known for promoting sleep (e.g., lavender, chamomile, hops)
- Optional: rice or flaxseed for weight
- String or ribbon
- Scissors

**Steps:**
- If using fabric squares, fold them in half and sew two sides to create a pouch, leaving one side open.
- Mix your chosen dried herbs. A good combination might be:
    - 2 parts lavender
    - 1 part chamomile
- If desired, add a small amount of rice or flaxseed to give the sachet some weight.
- Fill your pouch about 2/3 full with the herb mixture. Don't overfill, as you want the scent to be able to permeate.
- If using a pre-made pouch, simply tie it closed with string or ribbon.
- For sewn pouches, fold the open edge inward and sew it closed, or tie it with string if you prefer.
- Optional: Decorate your sachet with embroidery or attach a label with the contents.

To use, place the sachet under your pillow or nearby on your nightstand. The gentle aroma of the herbs can help promote relaxation and better sleep. Refresh the herbs every few months or when the scent fades.

**How to make your own bath blend:**

**Materials:**
- 1 cup Epsom salt (optional)
- 1/2 cup sea salt or Himalayan pink salt
- 1/4 cup baking soda
- 1/4 cup dried herbs (e.g., lavender, rose petals, chamomile)
- 10-15 drops essential oils (choose based on your desired effect and make sure it's safe to use on skin!)
- Large mixing bowl
- Spoon for mixing
- Airtight glass jar for storage

**Steps:**
- In a large bowl, combine the Epsom salt, sea salt, and baking soda. Mix well.
- Add your chosen dried herbs to the salt mixture. Crumble them slightly to release more of their scent.
- Add 10-15 drops of your chosen essential oils. Some relaxing options include lavender, chamomile, or ylang-ylang. For an energizing blend, try peppermint or citrus oils.
- Mix all ingredients thoroughly, ensuring the oils and herbs are evenly distributed. Transfer the mixture to an airtight glass jar for storage.
- To use: Add 1/4 to 1/2 cup of your bath blend as you fill your tub.

**Tips:**
- Keep the blend dry until use to preserve its potency.
- If you prefer not to have loose herbs in your bath, you can put the blend in a muslin bag before adding it to the water.
- Always test for any skin sensitivities, especially when using new essential oils.

So, this is totally doable, and it's such a lovely activity to enrich your life. You know, to make your own... *anything*: your own medicine, your own food, your own... whatever. It's empowering, it's a meaningful step away from the mass consumerism out there, and it will help you so much to feel connected to this world.

There's this quote I stumbled upon a while ago:

*"I think millennials are going to be the generation that simply tried to make it work. They couldn't afford the 100 acres, so they had to make do in their own backyward. They finally realised that the scheme of convenience was making them sicker and sadder, day by day. So they became more self-sufficient. And they discovered traditions of old that were never taught to them, and brought them back to life. They're starting to find the joy in simplicity, running away from the unsustainable pace being set by the rest of society. I think they'll be known as the generation who finally found a sense of peace in the heed of constant news cycles and cultural panic at every corner, I think this generation will finally be the one that took us back to a much, much better way of life."*

- Unkown

That is the journey we are on, wild ones...

## Reflection Questions:
- When you imagine your future self, how does she use herbs and plants in her daily life?
- How do you currently relate to healing? Do you outsource it, or do you trust your own instincts?
- Which remedies or products would you love to replace with your own creations first?
- How does it feel to think of caring for yourself with things you have made by hand?
- Do you remember anyone in your family or ancestry who worked with herbs? How might you be continuing their thread?

## Further Reading & Inspiration:
- "The Herbal Medicine-Maker's Handbook" by James Green (A practical guide on making tinctures, salves, teas, and more. Very hands-on)
- "Herbal Magick" by Annabel Margaret, aka The Green Witch (Explores the spiritual and magical uses of herbs in ritual, spell work, and everyday practice)
- Online resources and videos by Annabel Margaret (approachable demonstrations that show how simple tools and herbs can become powerful allies)
- Local herbalists and community workshops (wherever you live, seek out small workshops or community classes; learning in person can give you confidence and connection)

**Your space for notes, doodles & drawings:**

# You were meant to be wild.

# Unplugging from social media: a wild return to presence

If you're anything like me, your phone is probably never far from reach. Notifications buzz, the screen lights up, and before you know it, you've fallen into the familiar scroll. Social media has become an almost unquestioned part of modern life. It promises connection, visibility, and opportunity, yet leaves so many of us feeling drained, distracted, and oddly disconnected from ourselves.

## The catch-22 of being online

As a writer, I've wrestled with this contradiction firsthand. Books invite slowness, solitude, and deep attention, while platforms like Instagram or TikTok are fuelled by speed and distraction. To succeed in publishing today, I was told, an author must be online. It felt like a catch-22: in order to share stories meant to help people unplug, I needed to plug in even more.

But this tension, of course, is not unique to authors. Anyone working or creating today faces the same paradox: the tools that promise connection often erode the very qualities (authenticity, peace, creativity) we want to nurture. The Netflix documentary *The Social Dilemma* highlights this uncomfortable truth: social platforms are not neutral tools. They are engineered systems of manipulation, designed to keep us scrolling, hooked on dopamine hits from likes and comments. What looks like communication is often just exploitation of our attention.

## Rewilding our attention

Rewilding is not just for forests, rivers, and open skies; it is also about reclaiming our inner landscapes. Social media scatters our attention across thousands of voices, but the wild calls us to reclaim focus, depth, and presence. Every moment we choose to look at the sky instead of a screen, or walk without headphones, we are rewilding our attention.

The truth is, we don't need to know what thousands of complete strangers are doing. We don't need to perform every beautiful moment for an audience. A sunset is still a sunset even if it isn't posted. A walk in the woods remains sacred whether or not it is recorded, probably even more so. Rewilding is remembering that our lives are whole and meaningful without digital applause.

## The feminine way of Being

For women in particular, social media can magnify the old patterns of performance. We are praised for visibility, for beauty, for "content" rather than substance. Many inspiring female writers have admitted they felt a deep sense of relief when age finally freed them from the male gaze, when they became "invisible" and could live for themselves instead of performing. Rewilding invites us into that freedom now. It gives permission to step outside without makeup, to resist the pressure to be "on display," and to live from integrity rather than comparison.

And paradoxically, it also offers space to finally *be seen* in a truer sense: not through filters and algorithms, but through authentic presence in our own bodies and our own lives. The feminine energy does not chase likes or hustles for attention. It knows how to receive, attract, and savour joy in the process of creation. Rewilding means choosing **being over doing**.

## A different kind of connection

The good news is that there are other ways to connect and create without giving our energy away to platforms that deplete us. A personal website, a blog, a newsletter, Pinterest: these are all slower, gentler forms of connection. They attract readers or friends who are genuinely searching for what you offer, not mindlessly scrolling past. They also belong to you, unlike social accounts that can vanish with the next algorithm change.

And most importantly, we need to remember that there is the quiet community. Not everyone comments or likes. Many people simply read, watch, or quietly absorb. Trusting that quiet presence, those invisible readers or supporters, is resisting the demand for constant performance. It is recognising the value of connection that doesn't need to be measured in numbers.

## A rewilding practice: unplugging

You don't need to delete every app tomorrow, but you can begin to treat social media as the exception rather than the rule. Build in technology breaks. Delete apps when they drain you. Step outside without your phone and experience the wild moment fully. Curate your digital environment with the same care you might bring to your physical home, choosing only what nourishes. The unfollow-button is your best friend.

Rewilding means asking: what would life feel like if I stopped chasing and allowed myself to just *be*? How much more creativity, rest, and joy might be possible if I stopped scattering my attention across a thousand timelines and instead rooted it here, in my own story, my own land, my own life?

Because rewilding is not only an outward journey into forests and rivers. It is an inward reclamation of time, focus, and presence. And perhaps one of the bravest ways to rewild in the modern world is to gently, consciously, unplug.

# nature journaling

## Discovering the magic in your own backyard

A notebook can become a doorway. With a pen or a pencil in your hand, the ordinary world begins to shift. When you write, you capture impressions, stories, and fleeting thoughts. When you draw, something else happens: your attention lingers. To sketch a leaf or trace the curve of a feather, you have to slow down enough to notice its edges, its textures, its small imperfections. And in that slowing, your perception deepens.

Writing sharpens memory, while drawing sharpens presence. Together they transform a simple journal into a living record of your relationship with the earth around you. A sparrow on the fence, the moss on the stone, the clouds tumbling at dusk… those are all details that might once have slipped by unnoticed, but they become companions once they're written or drawn onto the page.

You don't need wilderness to begin. A backyard, a balcony, or a single tree outside your window can hold more layers of magic than you expect. With each entry, you strengthen your bond with place and train your senses to notice what has always been there.

## How to get started:

**Choose your notebook:** Pick one that feels comfortable to hold and easy to carry. It doesn't need to be fancy, but it should invite you to open it often.

**Gather your tools:** A pencil, pen, or small watercolour set is enough. Use what you already have. The goal is consistency, not perfection.

**Step outside:** Sit in your yard, on your balcony, or near a window. Notice one small detail that draws your eye. A leaf, a shadow, a bird. Begin there.

**Write before you draw:** Jot down the date, time, and what stands out to you first. Capture scents, colours, or movements. Let your words map your surroundings.

**Sketch what you see:** Spend a few minutes tracing outlines, shapes, or textures. Don't worry about accuracy. Focus on staying present with what you observe.

**Return often:** Visit the same place at different times of day or through the seasons. Each entry builds a conversation between you and your landscape.

**Reflect on the changes:** Read back over past pages. Notice what has shifted outside and within you. The record becomes not only of nature, but of your own attention.

## Don't make my mistake

I'll be honest: I struggled with this practice. Perfectionism has always been my trap, especially with anything artistic. I can be so hard on myself that I give up before I even begin. It's the same reason I didn't start writing novels until my thirties. I tried many times before, but the gap between what I imagined and what appeared on the page was unbearable. Instead of pushing through that awkward, imperfect stage, I walked away.

For years, I poured my energy into what I now think of as a shadow career. I became a travel writer, capturing my own experiences instead of learning the craft of fiction. It was satisfying in some ways, but the real dream waited in the background. When the pandemic came and travel stopped, I had no excuse left. I had to turn toward the work I'd been avoiding for so long. As painful as that time was, it gave me the reset I needed.

The same pattern repeated itself when I sat down with my nature journal. I had visions of the beautiful field sketches and painted pages I'd saved on Pinterest – pages by naturalists and artists I admire. My first attempts looked nothing like theirs. One morning I took my journal out to the porch, determined to draw the plants and trees in my own garden. Within minutes I felt defeated. Capturing their light and shadow, their dimensions and delicate details, was overwhelming. I nearly gave up. I was ready to close the book and tell myself I had failed this month's practice. But then I remembered something essential: a nature journal is not meant to be a "portfolio". It isn't for social media. It isn't a product to perfect or sell.

A nature journal is a conversation with the living world, and the only person it needs to serve is *you*.

## A nature journal is just for you.

A nature journal is just that: It is a *journal*. It is a documentation, a private documentation, of your rewilding journey, of your relationship with the plants and the trees and the flowers. It doesn't have to be perfect. In fact, there is a beauty in it not being perfect.

And so, I went back out there, and I really sat with… being bad at creating. And I've found this video by Ed Sheeran the other day, and Ed Sheeran says a similar thing, and that is that: Artists are not born, they are *made*. And they are made by practicing, by going through lots and lots of art that sucks, and getting better at it is all about being able to sit with the bad art, knowing that the quicker you get all the bad art out of your system, the sooner the quality art will appear on the page. And with the nature journal, all of that doesn't even matter necessarily. Because it's such a personal, private thing.

A nature journal is you, *thinking on paper*. It's a way for you to connect and sit with the nature that surrounds you. A way to document and notice the changes that happen in your area throughout the year. The observations that you make, the questions that you're wondering about, and the connections you make between things. And there is another thing I've realised, and I think this is such a beautiful lesson to learn from this: For me, nature journalling is the perfect hack to get me to pay closer attention to the world around me, to get out of my head and interact with nature on a deeper level, to get quiet and become aware.

### And here comes the brilliant twist:

The art, then, is *in support of* paying attention to nature. You see, so often, artists will say that their art was *inspired by* nature. But with nature journalling, it's the other way around. And because of that, if you draw something, and it's not "pretty" – that's okay! Because it was never about the art, it's about you noticing. And when you drew something that's not living up to your standards, all you should take from that is the permission to try again and make another one. And over time, you're creating this beautiful journey on paper, and you will see progress, and you will see how you got better. And this is something I've been doing for the longest time, actually: I like to go back to the beginning of an artist I admire. I love to watch YouTube videos of Ed Sheeran, busking in the streets. I love to read V.E. Schwab's early works, or when I find a creator I adore on social media, I like to scroll down to their earlier posts, to see how much they've learnt. Nobody starts out perfect. And the other thing is that, with creative endeavours, it happens very quickly that our work becomes our whole life. A quote by Helena Bonham Carter comes to mind:

*"I think everything in life is art. What you do. How you dress. The way you love someone, and how you talk. Your smile and your personality. What you believe in, and all your dreams. The way you drink your tea. How you decorate your home. Or party. Your grocery list. The food you make. How your writing looks. And the way you feel. Life is art."*

And while that is so true and beautiful, some art deserves to be private, deserves not to be shared, deserves to be only for you. And your nature journal might be one of those things. It's your own private journey of becoming a naturalist – not to make a career out of it, but simply because it enriches your life, your every-day-little-life. It's a great way of helping yourself become more curious about the world around you. And the more you do it, the more those little mysteries start pulling you deeper and deeper into everything that's going on out there, and you'll be amazed just how much unexpected beauty you might find in a feather or a leaf or a flower.

It's… it's very small. It's very quiet. And it's very, very personal. It's an incredibly grounding practice that helps deepen your understanding of the natural world that's right outside your doorstep. That is what Rewilding is all about: It's to feel at home in this world, to feel like you belong, that you're a part of what's going on around you, and that there is a reason why you landed where you landed in this world. I truly believe that the place you feel at home, be that the country you were born in or that "heart place" you chose to make your home as you grow older, this stuff is not random. There is a design to it, and you, being in that place, you matter there.

## Reflection Questions:
- Do you allow yourself to create without worrying how it looks, or do you feel pressure to perform?
- What shifts when you focus on observation rather than making something beautiful?
- How might your life enrich if you noticed the small details in your garden, on your way to work, or local park that you might otherwise have walked past?

## Further Reading & Inspiration:
- Keeping a Nature Journal by Clare Walker Leslie (a practical, gentle guide that shows how observation and sketching can deepen your relationship with the natural world.)
- The Laws Guide to Nature Drawing and Journaling by John Muir Laws (for when you want to dive deeper into techniques, light, and colour).
- Ira Glass's talk on creativity and "the gap" (search for the video online to hear it in his own words. It's a balm for anyone struggling with perfectionism.)
- Pinterest boards or Instagram feeds of field sketchers and naturalists (use them not as a standard to measure yourself against, but as sparks of inspiration to fuel your own practice.)

**Your space for notes, doodles & drawings:**

# All The Beauty That I See

In the chaos of our modern ways,
Amidst the noise and endless craze,
I sometimes long for simpler times,
When joy was found in simpler rhymes.

I seek the solace of the trees,
The rustle of leaves, the gentle breeze,
To ease my mind, to calm my soul,
And find a sense of being whole.

For in the quiet of Nature's hand,
I find a peace that helps me stand
Against the rush of daily life,
And all the worries, stress and strife.

So, I learn to cherish every tree,
And all the beauty that I see,
It's in these moments that I can find
A joy that's pure and unconfined.

# healing the land

## Community & Country

At the beginning of this book, I included an acknowledgement of the Wadandi people, the traditional custodians of the land on which I live and write. Their presence, their wisdom, and their connection to this place is something I carry with me every day.

As a relatively new Australian (I've been here for five years now), one of the great joys of moving here has been learning from Aboriginal culture. It was a huge draw for me, something that pulled me toward this continent and made me want to root myself here. Aboriginal people have lived with, and cared for, this land for over 60,000 years. Their relationship to "Country" is literally familial. Country is mother, kin, ancestor, and teacher all at once. It is sung to, cared for, listened to, and loved.

Rewilding isn't a personal journey, separated from the whole. If anything, it is the journey back to remembering that we are part of the whole. Rewilding, then, also involves looking *outward*, caring for the earth beneath our feet, and for the community around us. This practice is where the two threads of rewilding, self and land, intertwine most clearly. To heal ourselves, we must also tend to the places we inhabit. To belong, we must learn how to listen to the land and the people who have walked before us.

That is what guided me into this month of my rewilding year: a commitment to weave myself more deeply into the place I now call home, through community and through Country.

## Finding home

For most of my adult life, "home" has been a restless concept. I've lived in different countries, moved frequently, and for years felt more like a nomad than someone rooted in place. By consciously engaging with both the land and the people here, I began to feel at home in a way I never had before.

It was the act of participating, of joining in, listening, and showing up. Attending local events, meeting other writers and neighbours, volunteering for projects, but also spending quiet time walking these paths has deepened my belonging. What once felt temporary has started to feel permanent. My feet are sinking into the soil, and my heart is beginning to recognise this land as kin as well.

Falling in love with a place is a slow unfolding. Each birdcall, each shift of season, each encounter with community adds another thread to the tapestry. And through this practice, you too might realise that belonging is not something you wait for, but something you create by actively weaving yourself into the life of a place.

## Wisdom from the Wadandi People

One of the most profound gifts of living here has been learning from the Wadandi people, who have cared for this land for tens of thousands of years. Their relationship with Country is unlike anything I grew up with in Europe. Country, in their view, is not property to be owned. It is a living relative, one that nourishes, shelters, teaches, and must in turn be respected and cared for.

This perspective carries such humility. To walk on Country is to enter into relationship, to listen, to tread lightly. A perspective that shifts how you move through the world: less as a consumer of resources, and more as a participant in a living system.

When they speak of Country, they speak of belonging. Belonging to the earth, to the waters, to the seasons, to the spirits of place. The lesson is clear: when we care for the land, the land cares for us.

This wisdom has become a cornerstone of my rewilding practice. It reminds me that healing myself and healing the earth are inseparable. And it inspires me to take small steps every day to nurture this bond, whether through ritual, conservation, or simply listening more closely when the wind carries its stories.

## Reconnecting with Country in my own life

During this month, I made it my intention to move beyond theory and to actually live into the practice of reconnecting with Country. What unfolded was a series of moments that deepened not only my sense of place but also my sense of belonging.

I attended the local Writers Festival in Margaret River, where I spent a weekend surrounded by other storytellers (this is a great example why you should spend some time at the beginning of your year to roughly plan when to do what practice: I deliberately chose May for my Community & Country month, knowing that's when the festival would be on). On the surface, this was about books and publishing, but beneath it all, it was an act of community, of gathering, listening, exchanging, and celebrating voices rooted in this land. It reminded me that rewilding isn't always solitary; it thrives in connection.

I also signed up for citizen science projects during my month, logging sightings of endangered black cockatoos and beach-nesting birds. These simple acts – pausing to notice, recording, and contributing to collective knowledge – gave my daily walks a larger meaning. I was no longer a passerby in the landscape, but a participant in its care.

One of the most moving experiences was walking with a Wadandi Elder. He showed us how to make fire, pointed out plants with healing properties, and spoke of Country as a living being. The way he honoured the land, with songs, stories, and reverence, left a deep imprint. For the Wadandi, even tools and crafts are infused with spirit, made with the awareness that everything carries life and meaning. That worldview has changed how I look at even the simplest things in my own home. Every object carries its own kind of magic.

And in quieter moments, I picked up my camera and wandered with my husband Frank through the bush, capturing the patterns of light and shadow, the curl of leaves, the flight of birds. Photography became a way of paying attention to Country, of holding still long enough to see.

All of these experiences, some grand, others ordinary, were strands in the same weave: returning to relationship with land, people, and spirit. They were reminders that home is not simply where we live, but how we live in connection with place.

## Your path to reconnection

Wherever you live, you have your own Country, the land, waters, skies, and seasons that hold you. Reconnection doesn't always come through big or dramatic acts. It often begins with attention, respect, and small rituals of care. Here are some ways you can start:

**Learn local history and folklore:** Begin by discovering the stories of the land beneath your feet. Who cared for this land before you? What traditions, songs, or practices guided their lives? Many regions also carry pagan or folk customs connected to the cycles of the year. Knowing this heritage roots you more deeply in place and helps you see your surroundings as layered with meaning.

**Spend more time outdoors:** Step outside and linger. Walk in your local park, along a riverbank, or even around your neighbourhood. Notice which birds return in different seasons, which trees bloom, and how the light shifts through the months. A simple guidebook to local flora and fauna can help turn your curiosity into deeper knowledge.

**Artistic engagement:** Creativity is one of the most powerful ways to connect with land. Keep a nature journal (see previous practice), sketch leaves or clouds, write small poems, or photograph the same tree throughout the year. These things train you to notice, and through noticing, you begin to build relationship.

**Seek local experts:** Look for people who know your land well. This could be Indigenous Elders, park rangers, herbalists, or teachers offering survival training or plant identification courses. Learning from others not only deepens your knowledge but also places you within a community of caretakers.

**Celebrate seasonal changes:** Marking the turning of the seasons is a beautiful way to honour the rhythm of life around you. You might follow pagan festivals, Indigenous calendars, or simply create your own small rituals, lighting a candle at solstice, walking barefoot at the first spring rain, cooking a seasonal meal. These moments remind you that you too are part of nature's cycle.

**Gardening:** Cultivate even the smallest relationship with the land. If you have a garden, plant native species that support local wildlife. If you live in an apartment, grow herbs on your windowsill or care for a single plant. Tending to life, however small, is a way of grounding yourself.

**Collect natural treasures:** Pick up feathers, shells, or stones that catch your eye on walks. Place them on a small altar, desk, or windowsill as reminders of your bond with the land. These little talismans carry memory and meaning, anchoring you back to the places where you found them.

Rewilding yourself and rewilding the land are not separate journeys. As you begin to honour the place you live, the land begins to feel like an ally. Over time, you'll find that the ground beneath your feet is something you belong to.

## Reflection Questions:
- When you think of the land beneath your feet, what stories (personal, historical, or cultural) come to mind?
- What does Country mean to you, in the place where you live?
- How does your body feel when you spend time outdoors in your local environment?
- Are there seasonal rhythms you already notice? How might you celebrate or honour them more consciously?
- What practices help you feel most connected to land?
- In what ways could you give back to the land that sustains you?

## Further Reading & Inspiration:
- Bruce Pascoe: Dark Emu (A transformative book on Aboriginal land practices in Australia, challenging common myths and revealing a deep culture of farming, fire management, and care for Country.)
- Robin Wall Kimmerer: Braiding Sweetgrass (A beautiful weaving of Indigenous wisdom, botany, and personal story, showing how reciprocity with land creates both abundance and belonging.)
- Local citizen science projects: Many regions have bird counts, wildlife surveys, or conservation programs you can join. These create hands-on opportunities to give back to land while learning.
- Seasonal calendars: Look for Indigenous seasonal calendars (if available in your area) or folk traditions that guide planting, harvesting, or rituals.

**Your space for notes, doodles & drawings:**

# How to heal the sister wound, and why it's so important that we do.

Every woman knows the feeling. The quiet unease when another woman enters the room and something inside tightens. The subtle competition that begins before either of you says a word. The comparison that hums beneath the surface of friendship. These are familiar scenes. They happen in workplaces, families, and friendships, often without malice, yet they leave a residue of mistrust.

That tension has a name: the sister wound.

The sister wound is the inherited pain and mistrust that women often carry toward one another. It shows itself in jealousy, comparison, judgment, and the urge to compete rather than connect. It's the inner voice that says, "She's prettier," or "She's doing better," or "I need to prove myself." These thoughts may feel personal, but they are not born in isolation. They are echoes of a deeper fracture in our collective history.

## How the wound was created

Before patriarchal systems rose to dominance, women lived and worked in close community. They gathered food together, raised children together, and passed down knowledge about birth, medicine, and the cycles of the moon. This closeness created trust and interdependence. Each woman's strength supported the others. The success of one meant the wellbeing of all.

Then society changed. Power consolidated under male rule, and women's wisdom became a threat to the new order. The knowledge that once bound women together, healing, midwifery, herbalism, was declared dangerous. In the centuries of witch hunts that followed, the bond between women was deliberately torn apart. Survival often meant betrayal. A woman could save her life by accusing another. The message was clear: another woman could cost you everything.

That lesson lodged itself deep in our collective memory. Over generations, it turned into self-protection. Competing felt safer than trusting. Jealousy became a defence. The sister wound is the lingering scar of that long separation.

## How it still shows up

Modern life hides this wound beneath polished surfaces. It appears in social media comparisons, in subtle workplace rivalries, in the discomfort of female friendships that feel fragile instead of grounding. Even women who love other women deeply can sense its pull. The system rewards competition and speed, not collaboration or care. It praises individual success but rarely honours collective strength.

The sister wound thrives in environments that teach women to view each other through a lens of scarcity. If one woman wins, another must lose. If she is loved, admired, or chosen, that means someone else is not. This is how the wound keeps power in the hands of the system that caused it.

## Remembering what was lost

Healing begins with remembering that it wasn't always this way. Human history holds other ways of being. Women once lived by rhythms of collaboration. Their power was not about control but about connection—to each other and to the earth. They were healers, teachers, and guardians of life. Their work was to nurture, to protect, and to guide.

When that knowledge was erased, not only were women divided from one another, they were also divided from nature. The same mindset that feared female power began to dominate the natural world, seeing it as something to be controlled rather than respected. The wound between women mirrors the wound between humans and the earth.

## Steps toward healing:

**Acknowledge the wound:** Notice when feelings of competition or jealousy arise. Instead of judging them, ask what lies beneath. Often these moments reveal a hidden longing—a part of you that wants to grow or to feel seen. Awareness is the first act of healing.

**Celebrate other women:** When another woman succeeds, let her success expand your sense of what's possible. Her light does not dim yours. Support her courage and let it inspire you. Every time women celebrate each other, they weaken the old structure that once divided them.

**Rebuild community:** Healing the sister wound means creating new spaces of trust. Share knowledge. Listen without comparing. Offer help without keeping score. Build the kind of sisterhood our ancestors once knew, rooted in care and mutual respect.

**Reconnect with the living world:** The feminine and the natural are intertwined. Spend time outdoors. Notice the cycles of the moon, the change of seasons, the resilience of plants. These patterns remind us how to grow in balance instead of competition.

**Tell a new story:** Every conversation, every act of kindness between women, rewrites the narrative. Through art, writing, parenting, or friendship, we can tell stories of women who stand together rather than apart.

## Why this is part of Rewilding:

The Dalai Lama once said that the world will be saved by the Western woman. Perhaps he meant that women who have reclaimed a measure of freedom carry the responsibility to remember another way of living. Healing the sister wound is not a private task. It's part of healing the world. The way women treat one another mirrors how humanity treats the earth, either as competition or as kin.

Rewilding doesn't simply mean returning to nature, but also returning to our natural ways of being, ways that are cyclical, connected, and cooperative. The same conditioning that taught women to mistrust each other also taught humanity to dominate the natural world. Both arise from the same separation. To rewild as women means to remember what was forgotten: that we belong to one another, and that we belong to the earth.

When women reconnect with that instinctive bond, they stop playing by rules that were never made for them. They lead through rhythm, not hierarchy. They create from intuition, not competition. They care through reciprocity, not control. And in that shift, something larger can begin to heal, and that is the bond between humans and nature.

The sister wound can only close when women see one another as kin again, when each woman's rising strengthens the rest. That is how balance returns. That is how rewilding truly begins: when we remember that healing each other is inseparable from healing the earth.

## A wild body is a strong body

Rewilding the body means returning to the simple truth that your body is not an accessory, but your home, your vessel, your source of strength. For thousands of years, humans lived in rhythm with the land, walking long distances, foraging, carrying, climbing, resting under open skies. Our bodies are designed for movement, resilience, and vitality, yet so often they are confined, hidden, or neglected in the name of comfort or appearance.

To rewild your body is to treat it as part of nature, not something separate. It means learning to move in ways that make you feel alive and grounded, nourishing yourself with food that comes from the earth, and respecting your body as the incredible living system it is. It also means allowing yourself to be seen as you are, without make-up, without fashion, without the pressure to look "pretty." Your truest self is already whole, already enough.

This month's practice is an invitation to strengthen your body, honour its wisdom, and step into the kind of wild aliveness that has always been yours to claim.

## Lessons from the snowy owl

The idea for this month's practice came from a book that has been a steady companion on my rewilding journey: "Speaking With Nature" by Sandra Ingerman & Llyn Roberts. It's the book that first sparked the idea of devoting an entire year to rewilding, and in its pages, I came across a passage that stayed with me. It tells the story of the Snowy Owl, a magnificent bird of the far north of America.

As the ice caps continue to melt due to our changing climate, these owls are forced to migrate south in great numbers. They leave their Arctic home, where their white feathers kept them hidden against the snow, and they travel vast distances into unfamiliar landscapes. There, among the greens and browns of the forest, their snow-white plumage makes them stand out. Survival requires them to learn new ways of navigating, to adapt, to become visible in a way they have never been before.

That story resonates deeply. Because isn't that what rewilding often feels like? We step into new territory, sometimes dangerous, always unfamiliar, and suddenly we are seen. When you choose to show your true self to the world, when you let go of the camouflage you've carefully kept for years, it can feel both scary and freeing. Like the Snowy Owl, we are exposed… but also freer than before.

There is another lesson in the Snowy Owl's story, and it is the reason I chose this practice: strength. To travel those distances, to face the demands of a changing world, the owl cannot afford to neglect her body. She must care for herself, groom her feathers, keep her muscles strong, or she will not survive the journey.

We humans are nomadic by nature, too. Our bodies were shaped over millennia to move: to walk, to climb, to squat, to forage. And yet, I spend most of my days sitting at a desk. I try to vary it, sometimes standing, sometimes writing outside, but the truth is, the work always pulls me back into the chair. I knew I needed a counterbalance. I needed to find strength again in my body.

So, for this month, I committed to weight training. Each day, I stepped out onto my little porch, picked up my weights, and began to lift. It may not sound like the wildest practice, no running through forests or climbing mountains, but let me tell you: it is wild. To feel your own body grow stronger, to honour the vessel that carries you through life, to remember that we are animals too, built to move… there is nothing tame about that.

Before I share more, I want to make two things clear:

- This is not about getting thinner, nor is it about beauty. It's about *strength*, about honouring the body I've been given and keeping it capable for the years to come.
- Movement itself is a privilege. Health is a privilege. The older I get, the more grateful I am for every day that I can walk, stretch, or lift without pain.

## Strength as a form of Rewilding

For much of my life, I've lived in my head, writing stories, weaving characters, imagining worlds. My body was always second. But now, as part of this rewilding year, I am learning to bring the body forward. To give it the care and respect it deserves. And it starts here, with strength.

At first glance, lifting weights might not seem like the "wildest" practice. But in truth, reclaiming your strength is one of the most natural things you can do. Think of it as preparing your body to meet life with resilience. When you pick up a dumbbell, or even your own body weight, you're lowering your risk of chronic illness, improving your metabolism, balancing your hormones, and even supporting your mental health. For women, strength training also prepares the body for milestones such as pregnancy, childbirth, and the natural changes that come with age.

Here's something worth pausing over: muscle mass peaks at around 25. From then on, unless you actively work to maintain it, you lose 8–10% every decade.

Bone density follows a similar pattern, peaking in your early thirties before declining by up to 5% each year, depending on your stage of life. This is why strength training matters so much, especially as we grow older.

Strength also shapes how you move through the world. In a time when so many of us are hunched over screens, strength training restores posture. It helps you stand taller, with confidence and ease. This is rewilding in its purest form: reconnecting to the wisdom of the body and remembering that we are built to move.

And here's the encouragement I want to pass on to you: it's never too late. Start small, if you like, with light weights two or three times a week, even while you watch television. If your body is able to grow stronger, honour that gift. Out in nature, every animal stays fit because survival depends on it. And though we often forget it, we are animals too. **Movement is our birthright.**

The best way forward is to find the kind of movement that delights you. For me, running never felt right; it left me drained rather than nourished. Walking, on the other hand, has always been my joy. Back in Berlin, I was known for walking everywhere, no matter how long it took. Today, that love of walking has grown into long-distance hikes with my husband, a way to strengthen the body while connecting with nature.

The surprise of these past few weeks has been discovering how much I actually enjoy strength training. I can feel my body responding, growing steadier, stronger, more alive. And alongside strength, I'm reminded of the deeper truth: caring for the body also means tending to how we nourish it, how we rest it, how we respect it. Rewilding the body is a whole way of living, and strength is simply the beginning.

## Freeing yourself from the cage of beauty

For so many of us, our lives have been shaped by beauty. From the moment we were little girls, we learned (subtly or bluntly) that our worth was tied to how we looked. The way we dressed, the smoothness of our skin, the youth in our faces: all of it became a performance under the constant gaze of others. Patriarchy has thrived on this performance, keeping women busy with appearance so we would have less energy to live fully in our own truth.

And yet, many women have spoken of the relief that comes with age, when the spotlight of beauty begins to fade. Writers like Margaret Atwood, Gloria Steinem, and Ursula K. Le Guin have all written about this transition. Le Guin, in particular, described the freedom of invisibility; how growing older meant she no longer felt bound to the expectations that once weighed heavily on her. She wrote of being liberated from the male gaze, and how invisibility opened a new way of living more authentically (as written by Le Guin's in her essay "69. The Diminished Thing", May 2013).

Rewilding your body can begin here. It can look like walking out the door without make-up, without the daily armour, without the quiet voice that tells you to "make yourself pretty first." It can mean refusing to perform your life for anyone else's approval. It can mean remembering that your body is not an object to be looked at, but a living, breathing force of nature.

Paradoxically, rewilding can also mean the opposite: stepping fully into your own visibility for the first time. Maybe for you, rewilding is not hiding but finally being seen. Not for conforming to someone else's idea of beauty, but for showing up in your own skin, proud and confident. To walk into the world knowing your body carries strength, wisdom, and experience that needs no apology.

Whether invisibility feels like freedom, or visibility feels like courage, the heart of it is the same: **you get to decide how you inhabit your body.** Rewilding asks you to notice where you have been shaped by other people's expectations and where you might be ready to release them. It asks you to stand in your body not as the vessel of your wild, sovereign life.

## Practices to rewild your body this month

Rewilding your body does not mean overhauling your entire life in one go. It means making space for small, steady shifts that help you return to your natural strength and freedom. Here are some ways you can begin:

**Move Every Day in a Way That Feels Good:** This could be strength training with light weights, a yoga flow, or a long walk in the park. The important thing is consistency: show up for your body daily, even if it's only ten minutes.

**Get Into Squatting-Mode:** One of the easiest and best ways to return your body to its natural state is by practicing its most natural resting state: Squatting. Squatting is how humans have always rested, eaten, worked, and given birth. To begin, spend one minute a day in a gentle squat, supporting yourself if needed, and increase the time gradually until you can rest comfortably for ten minutes by the end of thirty days.

**Step Outside Without Make-Up:** Try going for a walk, running errands, or meeting a friend without covering your face. Notice what comes up: discomfort, freedom, relief… and hold space for it.

**Practice Standing Tall:** Throughout the day, check your posture. Roll your shoulders back, lift your chest, and feel how it changes your mood and confidence. This small practice reminds your body of its strength.

**Lift Something Heavy:** If you have weights, wonderful. If not, fill a backpack with books or use water bottles. Lifting builds muscle, bone density, and confidence, reminding you that your body is capable.

**Nourish Yourself Well:** Notice what you're putting into your body. Eat food that energises you, drink water consciously, and treat eating as a way of honouring your body's wild intelligence.

**Give Thanks to Your Body:** At the end of each day, pause for a moment of gratitude. Thank your body for carrying you, for breathing, for moving. Even if it aches, even if it struggles, it is your home.

## Reflection Questions:
- When do you feel most at home in your body?
- What messages did you grow up with about how a woman "should" look, and how are they still shaping you today?
- How does it feel to move your body with the goal of strength rather than focusing on appearance?
- When you go outside without make-up or effort, what emotions come up? Freedom? Vulnerability? Both?
- Where in your daily life can you choose strength over perfection, health over performance?
- How might you celebrate your body as it is, not as you've been told it should be?

## Further Reading & Inspiration:
- Sharon Blackie: If Women Rose Rooted (A powerful weaving of myth, landscape, and women's voices, reminding us of the deep connection between female strength and the land.)
- Sharon Blackie: Hagitude: (An inspiring look at the gifts of aging, with mythic archetypes that free us from patriarchal expectations and offer a rewilded vision of womanhood.)
- Sandra Ingerman & Llyn Roberts: Speaking with Nature (Beautiful wisdom stories, including the Snowy Owl, that link human life to the rhythms of the wild world.
- Clarissa Pinkola Estés: Women Who Run With the Wolves (A classic work of feminist mythology, exploring the instinctual, untamed side of the feminine that lives in all of us.)

**Your space for notes, doodles & drawings:**

# Granddaughters Of Witches

We are the granddaughters of the witches you failed to burn,
Wild and fierce, our spirits free and unconcerned.
We roam the forests and swim in the streams,
Gathering herbs and weaving magic in our dreams.

We dance in the moonlight, our hair wild and long,
Singing songs of the earth, our connection, oh so strong.
We are the women who rewild and reclaim
The knowledge and power that history tried to defame.

We gather in circles, our voices calm and clear,
Honouring the ancestors and all those who came here.
We learn from each other, our wisdom deep and true,
We heal ourselves and the earth with all that we do.

We are the granddaughters of the witches you failed to burn,
And we are the women who will never return
To the ways of the past that tried to control,
For we are wild and free, and that's how we'll grow.

# studying the sky

## Lessons from up above

For this month's practice, your invitation is to look up. To pause, tilt your face to the heavens, and reconnect with the vastness that stretches endlessly above you. The sky is our oldest teacher – sun, moon, stars, and shifting clouds have guided human life since the dawn of our species. Our ancestors planted, harvested, navigated seas, and told stories by the movements of the sky. To rewild ourselves means to rekindle that connection, to step back into a rhythm where the sky is not a backdrop but another companion we can turn to.

This practice is deceptively simple: sunrise, sunset, nightfall. A few minutes each day of watching, of noticing, of remembering. Because you already carry this knowledge in your bones, that awe of standing under a starry night, the comfort of dawn's first light. What is missing is the space to make it a priority.

When was the last time you stood in silence as the stars revealed themselves one by one? When did you last allow yourself to be humbled by a sky so wide it makes your worries feel small? To study the sky is to remember your place in the cosmos, to open yourself to lessons written not in books but in light and shadow, movement and stillness.

## Remembering our ancestors' sky

Rewilding is, at its core, a return to a more natural state of being. When I think of our ancestors, I imagine how deeply connected they were to the sky. With no Netflix, no phones, no constant distractions, the night sky must have been their greatest source of wonder. Picture them sitting around a fire, telling stories as stars wheeled above them. They would have noticed patterns, tracked the seasons, and asked themselves where they fit into this vast, magical display.

Personally, I believe they were more in tune with the intelligence of the Universe than we are today. If you live barefoot on the earth, rise with the sun, and sleep each night beneath the stars, you start to notice the subtleties, the rhythms and signs that guide you through life.

Many ancient cultures left traces of this profound connection. The Maya built temples and cities aligned perfectly with celestial events. Other civilisations, too, used the heavens as a map for both survival and meaning. You may have heard the theories – controversial, yes, but compelling nonetheless – of Graham Hancock ("Ancient Apocalypse" on Netflix) and others who suggest there might once have been an advanced civilisation that lived in harmony with nature, not in opposition to it. Whether proven or not, the idea resonates deeply. Because what if, long ago, there were people who "got it right"? Who lived without harming the earth, who built with reverence rather than greed, whose story of progress was not expansion at all costs, but unity with the natural world? For me, this thought carries hope. Hope that we can imagine and create a new story for humanity, one in which we learn again from the sky.

## Watching the sunrise promotes healthy circadian rhythm

Coming back to watching especially the sunrise: When you expose yourself to early morning light, you support a healthy circadian rhythm, which helps you to get more restful sleep at night. And that is because of the wavelengths at sunrise and sunset, which have the biggest impact on those parts in our brain that regulate our circadian rhythms, and also our mood and our alertness.

A study from 2017 found that people who were exposed to more light in the morning fell asleep more quickly at night and had fewer sleep disturbances compared to those who were exposed to less light in the mornings.

And on a more spiritual note, the colours of sunlight at rise and sunset are also especially helpful for activating the pineal gland, which is said to be the portal to divine wisdom.

## A sense that we are not alone

Looking up at the sky shifts the way worries and uncertainties are held. The vastness offers perspective: problems grow smaller, not in a dismissive way, but in the sense that they are part of something much greater. There is belonging in that feeling, a reassurance that all will be well. The same deep calm that arises when sitting quietly with an elephant.

The stars invite remembrance that we are woven into the fabric of the Universe. A higher intelligence hums through it all, carrying us, offering wisdom and perspective beyond what the mind or ego can grasp. Sorrows and struggles lose some of their weight when measured against such beauty, such immensity.

Sunrises and sunsets become teachers. They reveal that light and dark define each other, that neither is permanent. When the sun slips below the horizon here, it is rising somewhere else. This eternal rhythm restores trust in the timing of life, a faith that darkness always carries the seed of returning light.

## How you can reconnect with the sky this month:

**Begin and end your day with the sky:** Step outside or stand at a window at dawn or dusk, just for five minutes. Watch how the light changes. Notice the colours, the temperature, the way the world feels in those moments. Let sunrise and sunset become gentle anchors for your day. You might not do so *every* day this month, and that's okay. Remember, we are not aiming for perfection here.

**Make star-watching a ritual:** Lie on a blanket at night, turn off all distractions, and simply look up. You don't need to know the constellations; the act of gazing itself is enough. If you do want guidance, a simple stargazing app or a star map can help you name what you see.

**Track the moon's phases:** In combination with the moon-manifesting practice, start a simple moon journal or use the app I recommend in the moon-chapter to track your mood in relation to the moon phases. Over time, you may notice patterns in your energy, emotions, or sleep that align with the lunar cycle.

**Use the sky for perspective:** The next time you feel overwhelmed, pause and look up. Remember how small your worries are compared to the vastness above you. Let the sky hold the heaviness, even for a moment.

**Bring the sky indoors:** If you live in a city with light pollution, bring the sky into your space in other ways: hang star maps, keep a moon calendar, or light a candle each evening as a symbolic "sunset" ritual.

**Share the experience:** Invite a loved one to watch the stars with you or bring a child outside to look for the moon. Wonder is contagious, and shared awe deepens connection.

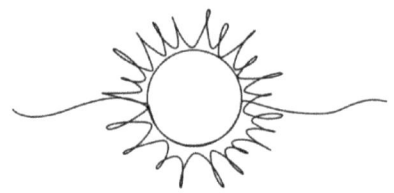

## Reflection Questions:
- When did you last notice a sunrise or sunset, and what feelings did it stir in you?
- How does watching the night sky shift your sense of perspective on your own life?
- What emotions or insights arise when you witness the cycles of the moon?
- Do you feel a connection between your inner rhythms and the rhythms of the sky?
- What childhood memories do you have of looking up at the stars? Can you bring that sense of wonder back into your life today?
- How might regular time with the sky restore trust in timing, cycles, and patience in your own journey?

## Further Reading & Inspiration:
- The Old Ways by Robert Macfarlane (lyrical explorations of paths, landscapes, and human connection to Earth and sky)
- The Power of Awe by Dacher Keltner (a fascinating dive into how awe transforms our wellbeing)
- Stargazing Apps/Star Maps (practical tools like Sky Guide or Stellarium to help you name the constellations and deepen your practice)
- Graham Hancock's "Ancient Apocalypse" series on Netflix

**Your space for notes, doodles & drawings:**

# Lost and Found

In this world of endless things,
And constant wants and needs,
I find myself at times adrift,
Lost amidst the endless greed.

But then I step outside my door,
And let my feet take me away,
To where the trees and rivers flow,
And nature holds the sway.

Here I find a different world,
One that needs no trinkets bold,
Just the gentle rustle of the leaves,
And the birdsong in the trees.

And in this simpler way of life,
I feel a joy that's unrefined.
I truly think I've found my place
In this serene and quiet space.

# wintering

## Learning how to truly rest

If you're anything like me, resting and doing less can feel almost impossible. But that's exactly what I want you to do over the coming weeks: learning to practice true rest. To guide me during my own practice, I had two wonderful companion books: "Wintering" by Katherine May and "Do Less" by Kate Northrup. Both were powerful in different ways. I underlined nearly every second sentence of "Wintering" and filled pages of notes while listening to the audiobook version of "Do Less". These books became gentle teachers, showing me why rest is not indulgence, but necessity. While you might feel called to these books as well, they are not necessary for this month's practice. In this chapter, I'll share with you three things:

- How to create more space for rest in your life
- What Northrup's concept of "egg wisdom" reveals about why doing less can lead to better results
- My own lessons from these weeks of wintering, and what I've learned in those dark and quiet stretches of life when everything seems to slow down.

A little disclaimer before we dive in: I am a happily childless, thirty-eight-year-old, self-employed author. Naturally, I don't carry the immense responsibility of keeping a small human alive. But like many self-employed people, I know the pressure of never fully switching off. Quitting the nine-to-five doesn't necessarily mean working less; it often means working twenty-four-seven.

This practice made me realise how little we truly know about resting. We talk endlessly about "work–life balance," boundaries, and self-care. Yet, when it comes to actually allowing ourselves to stop, to rest without purpose or performance, it feels nearly impossible. The moment I slow down, a voice rises inside me: What about that email you haven't answered? Shouldn't you be writing? Shouldn't you be doing something useful?

Humans are the only species that fights against this natural rhythm. Trees don't apologise for shedding their leaves. Bears don't feel guilty for hibernating. Yet, we humans push against our own need for stillness, as though pausing makes us less worthy.

There is a vast difference between taking breaks and truly resting. Scrolling through social media on the couch isn't rest. Answering emails in bed isn't rest. That's simply moving our busyness into a more comfortable position.

I remembered something from my safari guide training in South Africa. One afternoon, our teacher led us on a bush walk and, halfway through, he asked us to sit down under a tree. That was it. We stayed there the rest of the afternoon. No books, no phones, no conversation. At the time, I didn't fully grasp the gift of that exercise. Now I do.

True rest is the act of letting go, disconnecting from the need to produce, achieve, or prove. It's about giving your body and mind the space to simply be.

The constant demand we place on ourselves, especially as creatives or entrepreneurs, to stay in production mode is actually working against us.

## When everything goes dark

Our "winters" are these periods in our lives when everything seems to go dark – when we feel stuck, when we're waiting, when nothing seems to be happening on the surface. And instead of fighting against these periods, "Wintering" suggests we turn to Mother Nature and learn from her.

Because what winter, what nature, can teach us here is that, even when it looks like nothing is happening on the surface, that period of silence, of winter, of darkness, is actually an essential part of growth.

A seed doesn't apologise for taking time in the dark soil before it sprouts. The earth doesn't rush through winter to get to spring. There's important work happening in these quiet, dark times, work we can't see, but work that's absolutely necessary for what comes next.

This really hit home for me because as a creative, I often feel this immense pressure to always be visibly producing something. To have something to show for my time.

But (and I know this, in theory) creativity doesn't work like that. Ideas need time to compost. Stories need time to ripen. And sometimes, the most productive thing we can do is literally nothing.

So, let me tell you what happened over these past few weeks when I finally gave myself permission to embrace this. And I'll be honest: at first, it felt terrifying.

And so, the first few days of intentionally doing less really was like trying to speak a language I'd forgotten. And I kept catching myself reaching for my phone, making to-do lists, feeling guilty for "wasting time..." The hardest part was to allow that nothingness, that silence.

…But after a few days or so something interesting started happening: When I stopped filling every moment with mindless productivity, when I actually allowed myself to take walks without listening to podcasts, to sit and watch the Australian winter rain without the phone in my pocket, or reading those two books without so much as music playing in the background... my mind started doing this thing where it just wandered. And it was in that wandering that new ideas started showing up. Not because I was forcing them, but because I was finally giving them space to emerge.

What really surprised me and what might be very, very hard to admit is: The less I pushed myself to be productive, the more naturally productive I became. It's

like that paradox where the harder you try to fall asleep, the more awake you become. The moment you stop trying so hard, that's when sleep finds you.
And this is where Kate Northrup's concept of "egg wisdom" comes in, which has officially changed how I think about energy and output:

## "Egg Wisdom"

Northrup uses the metaphor of the egg to describe a woman's natural rhythm. A woman is born with all the eggs she will ever have. Each one waits, protected, until the time comes to be released. Unlike the sperm, which races and competes, the egg stays still. It sends a quiet magnetic signal that draws what is meant for it closer. The body knows this wisdom: creation does not come from chasing or striving, but from patience and readiness. When we slow down, we align with that truth. When we rest, we stop forcing outcomes and begin to attract what is already moving toward us. We are literally *designed to attract,* not chase.

Just like our bodies naturally know when to conserve and when to release energy, our creative lives have these same rhythms. But we've gotten so used to overriding these natural cycles, pushing through when we should be resting, forcing output when we should be gathering input.

Intentionally doing less is that rest isn't the opposite of productivity; it's actually the foundation of it. Just like winter isn't the opposite of growth – it's the season that makes growth possible.

Now, I want to be clear about something: doing less doesn't mean doing *nothing*. I still have to make sure I can pay my bills by the end of the month. But it means being much more intentional about where we put our energy. It means trusting that not everything needs to happen right now. It means understanding that some seasons are for output, and others are for input. Or, as I often say:

**Some years are for paddling; others are for riding the wave.**

Some seasons are for visible growth, and others are for the root work, the kind that happens beneath the surface where no one else can see it.

It feels almost rebellious to start the day not opening your laptop but opening a book instead. Because rest makes us vulnerable in a way that constant busyness does not. When we slow down, when we get quiet, that's when we start feeling all the things we've been too busy to feel.

## Where the magic happens.

I've noticed how my relationship with time has started to shift. Instead of seeing time as something to fill up, to maximise, to squeeze productivity out of, I'm learning to see it more like a landscape I move through. Some parts are steep hillsides that require more energy, and others are gentle valleys where I can catch my breath. And the more I practice this mindset, the more I notice how nature has been teaching us this lesson all along: The trees outside my window right now aren't trying to grow leaves in deep winter. They're not apologising for their bare branches. They're simply doing what they need to do in this season, and that's exactly what I'm learning to do, too.

So, let me share with you some practical things I've been experimenting with, and I want to acknowledge that what works for me might look different for you. But the point isn't to follow these exactly, but to find your own rhythm of rest and productivity:

First, I've started paying attention to my natural energy patterns throughout the day. When am I naturally more alert? When does my creativity peak? When do I start feeling foggy? And instead of fighting these patterns, I'm learning to work with them. For example, I've noticed that forcing myself to write in the afternoon never produces anything good. So, I've stopped trying and I'll do my admin work in the afternoon instead.

Second, I'm practicing what I call "intentionally not finishing." So, this means that I'll deliberately leave things unfinished sometimes, letting ideas simmer, allowing projects to rest. This is a great tip if you're a writer: When you finish work for the day, you want to leave your manuscript almost mid-sentence or mid-chapter, because it's much easier to come back to a work-in-progress the next day instead of starting with that dreaded "blank page".

Third, I'm redefining what counts as "productive time." Watching the birds outside my window for twenty minutes? That's productive, because it's letting my mind process and integrate. Taking a shower without trying to solve plot problems? That's productive; it's giving my brain the space it needs to work things out on its own. Cooking a meal slowly, paying attention to each ingredient, without multitasking or rushing? That's productive, because it's essentially a form of meditation that allows my thoughts to settle. Reading a novel purely for pleasure, without analysing the author's craft? That's productive too because it's filling up my creative well.

Learning to rest means tuning in to what your mind and body are telling you they need. And sometimes that means accepting that this particular day or week or month? Really isn't going to be your most productive one, and that's okay. Because just like nature needs winter to create spring, we need these quiet periods to create what comes next.

Lastly, I want to circle back to something Katherine May writes about in "Wintering" that really struck me. She talks about how these winter periods in our lives, whether they're literal or metaphorical, aren't something to "get through" or "survive." They're just another part of the cycle. They're where transformation happens.

And that's really what this month has taught me: Rest isn't simply the absence of work. It's not just what happens when we're too exhausted to keep going. Rest is active. Rest is necessary. Rest is productive in its own way.

The world won't fall apart when we slow down.
Our worth won't disappear if we take a break.
And sometimes, the most powerful thing we can do...

...is absolutely nothing at all.

## Reflection Questions:
- What thoughts or guilt tend to come up for you when you slow down?
- How does your body let you know that it's time to pause?
- Where in your daily life could you create small "wintering" moments of stillness and restoration?
- If you released the pressure to always be productive, what would you make space for?

## Further Reading & Inspiration:
- Katherine May, Wintering (A lyrical and honest reminder that darker, quieter seasons of life are not failures but invitations to heal, reset, and find new strength)
- Kate Northrup, Do Less (A powerful guide to working with your body's cycles, reclaiming rest, and allowing "egg wisdom" to show you how less effort can lead to greater alignment)
- Tricia Hersey, Rest Is Resistance (A manifesto that reframes rest as a radical, necessary act of reclaiming our humanity in a culture obsessed with productivity.)
- Tara Brach, Radical Acceptance (Encouragement to soften, pause, and rest into life as it is, instead of always striving.)

**Your space for notes, doodles & drawings:**

# Pitter-Patter

Soft pitter-patter

Raindrops on the sill

In this little moment

All the world stands still.

Grey skies overhead

But she feels the memory of sun

Joy in the small things,

Needing nothing, she's won.

Each drop a miracle

Of Nature's symphony

A moment in perfect harmony

With all that she has strived to be.

The calmness of the storm

A reminder to make space

A chance to slow down, slow,

And settle into her own pace.

The world outside, a constant brawl

But she has found her own delight

And for a moment, all is right

As she watches the rain fall.

# solo adventuring

## Your sacred closing ritual

If you've followed along this far, you've given yourself nearly a year of practices to rewild your body, your mind, and your spirit. Now comes the final step: your own adventure alone in the wild. Think of this as both a celebration and a sacred ritual, the moment where everything you've learned comes together.

Unlike the other practices, which you have scheduled in whatever order works best for you, this one is meant to happen at the end of your rewilding journey. It deserves time and space. Ideally, give yourself at least a few days away, a stretch long enough to shed the noise of your everyday life and hear the quieter voices within. You may need to book some time off work, arrange childcare, or shuffle your calendar. The very act of making that space is part of the ritual.

For me, a long-distance hike has always been the truest way to meet myself. Walking kilometre after kilometre with only the sound of my breath and the rhythm of my feet makes me feel both raw and alive. But if that isn't your thing, there are so many ways to create this adventure. You might book yourself a cabin tucked into the woods, camp beside a lake, or take a few days on the coast. The important thing is that you are alone, immersed in nature, and fully present with yourself.

I also want to say: don't let money hold you back. A solo adventure doesn't have to be expensive. Can you borrow a tent or a hiking rucksack from a friend? Could you pitch camp on someone's property by the lake or on a local trail for a night before heading further afield? What matters most is your intention to step outside of everything familiar and to meet yourself, stripped of distractions. Why alone? Because solitude is medicine. Out in the wild, with no one else to lean on, you become both student and teacher. You learn your own rhythms, your own fears, your own strengths. You remember that you are part of the natural world. And in that remembering, you discover a deeper trust in yourself, in the Earth, in your place within it all. This is the culmination of your Rewilding Year. A sacred rite of passage. A chance to close the circle in silent celebration, in solitude, and in the deep knowing that you are capable, strong, and utterly connected.

## A word on safety

Before you set off, let's talk safety. Solo adventuring is powerful precisely because it stretches you beyond your comfort zone, but it should never put you in real danger. The goal is to return home stronger, not to frighten yourself or others.

First, let someone you trust know where you are going and when you expect to return. Share your route if you're hiking, or the exact location of your cabin or campsite. Arrange a check-in, a simple text when you arrive, and another when you leave.

Second, be realistic about your skills and experience. If you've never hiked alone before, maybe start with a single overnight, choose a well-marked trail close to home, or consider working up to the challenge by going on daily hikes. If you're drawn to camping, but you've never set up a tent before, practice in your backyard first. Preparation is part of the ritual; it shows your body and your spirit that you're taking this seriously. Pack more food and water than you think you'll need. Bring layers for warmth, a good map, a charged phone or power bank, and a small first-aid kit. These small precautions make all the difference in allowing you to fully relax once you're out there.

And finally, listen to your intuition. If something feels off (a trail, a person, a campsite) trust yourself and turn back. It's also worth saying clearly: **this book cannot possibly cover outdoor safety, nor does it aim to do so.** Depending on where you live, your chosen landscape, and the length of your adventure, you may need to do additional research, whether that's learning basic navigation, familiarising yourself with local wildlife, or understanding weather patterns. In the Further Reading & Inspiration section you'll find some resources to help you deepen your knowledge before heading out.

## What to do when you're out there

Once you arrive at your chosen place, whether it's a forest trail, a quiet cabin, or a tent pitched under the stars, give yourself a moment to arrive fully. Breathe in the air, feel the ground beneath your feet, notice the sounds around you. This is not a trip to "get things done." This is your ritual of presence.

Here are some ways to make your time in solitude meaningful:

- **Begin with stillness.** Before you unpack, before you distract yourself with tasks, sit quietly. Let your body and mind catch up to the landscape. You might close your eyes and listen to the wind or water.
- **Create a rhythm.** Give yourself structure but keep it simple. A morning walk, an afternoon rest, an evening journal session. Rituals help you sink into the experience without the mind racing for entertainment.
- **Cook basic meals.** Choose simplicity over variety. Prepare food slowly, noticing textures and scents. Let the act of cooking itself become part of your grounding.
- **Work on your nature journal.** Record what you see, hear, and feel. Sketch a leaf, describe a sound, note a change in light. The goal is not perfection but presence.

## Reflection Questions:
- What surprised you most about yourself during this solo adventure?
- In what ways did solitude sharpen your connection to the land?
- Were there moments of discomfort or fear, and how did you move through them?
- What lessons from your Rewilding Year rose to the surface most clearly during this time?
- How do you want to carry the energy of this solo experience forward into your daily life?
- What part of your wild self do you feel ready to claim more fully?

## Further Reading & Inspiration:
- Wild: From Lost to Found on the Pacific Crest Trail by Cheryl Strayed (A powerful story of healing, loss, and self-discovery through solo hiking)
- Tracks by Robyn Davidson (An extraordinary account of walking alone across the Australian desert with camels, a reminder of courage and resilience)
- She Explores – www.she-explores.com (A community of women sharing stories of travel, adventure, and connection to the wild)
- Hiking Solo: A Woman's Guide to Safe (and Smart) Solo Hiking by Kelly King (Practical tips for safety and confidence on the trail)
- A Woman's Guide to the Wild by Ruby McConnell (Survival skills, safety strategies, and encouragement written specifically for women exploring the outdoors)

**Your space for notes, doodles & drawings:**

# Leaving It All Behind

I'm packing up to hit the road,
To leave behind my heavy load,
The weight of all my worries and my fears,
That I've been carrying all these years.

I'm leaving it all behind,
The stress, the strain, the daily grind,
To find a place where I can be,
Myself, unburdened, wild and free.

No more the crowded city streets,
No more the sound of rushing feet,
Instead, I'll wander through the fields,
Where Nature's beauty is revealed.

I'll find my peace in mountain views,
And in the beauty of ocean hues,
The gentle rustling of the trees,
And the buzzing of the bumblebees.

And in this newfound quietude,
I'll rediscover all that's good,
And leave behind what's holding me,
To find the person I can be.

I'll hit the road with my head held high,
And let the wind take me on by,
To get to a place where I can find
Freedom and some peace of mind.

# Letting go: How my own Rewilding Year came to an unexpected close

At the time I was meant to finish my own Rewilding Year, I found myself in bed with a nasty flu and the kind of jetlag that makes you question what century it is. I had planned an epic ending – the practice I had looked forward to most from the very beginning: a week-long solo journey into the Australian bush. It was going to be the culmination of everything I had learned, the perfect bookend to my Rewilding Year. Just me, my pack, and the Australian coast.

But instead of trekking through rough terrain, I was sipping tea and surrendering to what my body was telling me. At first, I wrestled with disappointment. Postponing was an option, of course, but something about extending the year into "a year and a month" didn't feel right. I had to sit with the feelings of failure, of not living up to my own expectation – and the vulnerability of having to admit it.

But then something within me clicked. I began to see that perhaps this was not failure, but the truest lesson of all. Because the deeper I reflected, the more I realised that this, in fact, *was* the perfect ending.

Nature is a master of surrender. Trees bend in storms rather than snapping. Rivers flow around obstacles instead of forcing their way through. Flowers close at dusk, trusting the sun to return.

This is surrender in action. This is resilience. And my body, too, was asking me to surrender, to rest, to withdraw, to pause. And hadn't I already been working on this? The month before had been dedicated to wintering, to the art of resting. Only then, rest had been *chosen*. This time, it was *demanded* of me.

I could now meet this involuntary pause with more grace. I could be gentle with myself. I could allow my body to rest, instead of trying to push through. And strangely, by letting go of my perfectly laid plans, I found myself in deeper alignment with the natural rhythms I had been studying all year.

We humans have built entire systems to resist nature. Artificial light to stretch our days, air conditioning to ignore the seasons, technology to override the body's signals. But rewilding asks us to let go of the illusion of control. To remember that we are part of nature. And sometimes the deepest rewilding happens not when we are out in the wild, but when we are forced to listen to our own body and surrender.

This practice of surrender runs deeper than simply honouring cycles of rest. It reaches into the way we live our entire lives. One book that has guided me through this, and that I re-read every year, is Michael Singer's "The Surrender Experiment." In it, Singer shares his decision to let go of his attachment to outcomes, to say yes to whatever life presented. He didn't become *passive*; he still acted with full commitment. But he stopped resisting or questioning what came his way. The result was extraordinary: from living as a hermit in the woods, he eventually became the founder of a billion-dollar public company. All because he surrendered to the flow of life rather than forcing his own plans. Singer's story illustrates what Nature has been showing us all along: that surrender is not weakness, but a profound form of trust. A fallen tree lets go of standing tall, and in doing so becomes home for fungi, insects, and new saplings. Rivers change course when blocked and create new valleys. The cycles of sun and moon remind us daily that darkness is followed by light. Nothing in Nature clings desperately to control.

And so, my final challenge – the one I had envisioned as a triumphant adventure into the wilderness – became instead a lesson in yielding. Not the ending I had planned, but perhaps the one I most needed.

Letting go was, in the end, the most rewilded act of all.

*(And for those wondering: yes, once I recovered, I did eventually head out on my solo adventure. It was quieter, perhaps less ceremonious than the grand finale I had imagined, but it was beautiful. And it reminded me once again that life's timing is rarely ours to dictate. We are always in partnership with something greater.)*

# Author's Note

Thank you, from the bottom of my heart, for walking alongside me through this Rewilding Year. Writing this book was both exhilarating and vulnerable, sharing pieces of my own journey in the hope that it might inspire yours.

If these practices helped you slow down, reconnect, or simply see the world with new eyes, then sharing them has been worth it. I hope you close this book – this year – feeling inspired to step a little more softly on the earth, and a little more gently with yourself.

If this book spoke to you, if it offered comfort, courage, or even one small spark of change, I would be so grateful if you took a moment to leave a review. Reviews are how books like this find their way into the hands of others who might need them, too. Think of it as passing on a torch: your words may become the light that guides someone else toward their own Rewilding Year.

Thank you again for your trust and your time. May the lessons of water, earth, sky, rest, and wildness continue to ripple through your days. And may you always remember you are part of nature, and you were meant to be wild.

With love and gratitude,

*Gisele Stein*

# Sources & Inspirations for this book

- Berendt, Joachim-Ernst. *The World Is Sound: Nada Brahma.*
- Blackie, Sharon. *Hagitude.*
- Blackie, Sharon. *If Women Rose Rooted.*
- Boland, Yasmin. *Moonology.*
- Brach, Tara. *Radical Acceptance.*
- Estés, Clarissa Pinkola. *Women Who Run With the Wolves.*
- Gaynor, Mitchell L. *The Healing Power of Sound.*
- Hersey, Tricia. *Rest Is Resistance.*
- Ingerman, Sandra & Roberts, Llyn. *Speaking with Nature.*
- Koniver, Laura. *The Earth Prescription.*
- May, Katherine. *Wintering.*
- Nichols, Wallace J. *Blue Mind.*
- Northrup, Kate. *Do Less.*
- Ober, Clinton; Sinatra, Stephen T.; & Zucker, Martin. *Earthing: The Most Important Health Discovery Ever!*
- Singer, Michael A. *The Surrender Experiment.*
- Tsui, Bonnie. *Why We Swim.*

Copyright © 2025 by Gisele Stein

All rights reserved.

www.giselestein.com

Stein Books & Publishing

1101 Hay Street, Suite #1031

West Perth,

WA 6005, Australia

No part of this book may be reproduced in any form or by any electronic or mechanical means, including information storage and retrieval systems, without written permission from the author, except for the use of brief quotations in a book review. This book is a work of fiction. The characters, incidents and dialogue are drawn from the author's imagination and are not to be construed as real. Any resemblance to actual events or persons, living or dead, is fictionalised or coincidental.

ISBN: 978-1-7635581-7-5

www.ingramcontent.com/pod-product-compliance
Lightning Source LLC
Chambersburg PA
CBHW041228240426
43661CB00013B/1165